Get Set for English Language

Titles in the GET SET FOR UNIVERSITY series:

Get Set for American Studies
ISBN 0 7486 1692 6

Get Set for English Language
ISBN 0 7486 1544 X

Get Set for English Literature
ISBN 0 7486 1537 7

Get Set for Geography
ISBN 0 7486 1693 4

Get Set for Linguistics
ISBN 0 7486 1694 2

Get Set for Media Studies
ISBN 0 7486 1695 0

Get Set for Philosophy
ISBN 0 7486 1657 8

Get Set for Politics
ISBN 0 7486 1545 8

Get Set for Study in the UK
ISBN 0 7486 1810 4

Get Set for English Language

Christine Robinson

Edinburgh University Press

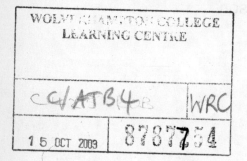
© Christine Robinson, 2003

Edinburgh University Press Ltd
22 George Square, Edinburgh

Typeset in Sabon
by Hewer Text Ltd, Edinburgh, and
printed and bound in Finland by
WS Bookwell

A CIP Record for this book is
available from the British Library

ISBN 0 7486 1544 X (paperback) V hm

CONTENTS

Key to main symbols   vii
Preface   ix
Introduction   xiii

PART I: WHAT IS ENGLISH LANGUAGE?

1 Phonetics and phonology: The sounds of English   3
2 Vocabulary   16
3 Inflectional morphology   29
4 Syntax   38
5 The history of English   62
6 Regional variation   81
7 Social variation   96
8 Functional variation   106
9 Language change   115
10 Language and poetry   126
11 And more   139

PART II: STUDY SKILLS IN ENGLISH LANGUAGE

12 Be in the know   149
13 Learning:
   reading, assessment and self-directed learning   152
14 Time management   158
15 Tutorials, seminars and oral presentations   161
16 Lectures   166
17 Essays and dissertations   168
18 Improving written communication   184
19 Examinations   201

APPENDICES

I: Sample degree exam paper   211
II: Sample essay with marker's comments   221

Index   231

KEY TO MAIN SYMBOLS

Consonants

Voiceless stops			Voiced stops			Nasal voiced stops		
[p]	as in	pat	[b]	as in	bad	[m]	as in	mum
[t]	as in	tap	[d]	as in	did	[n]	as in	nun
[k]	as in	clock	[g]	as in	gig	[ŋ]	as in	sing, think

Voiceless fricatives			Voiced fricatives		
[f]	as in	fat	[v]	as in	van
[θ]	as in	thigh, theta, breath	[ð]	as in	thy, that, breathe
[s]	as in	sip, hiss, cats	[z]	as in	zoo, buzz, dogs
[ʃ]	as in	ship, station	[ʒ]	as in	rouge, leisure
[h]	as in	hot			

Voiceless affricate			Voiced affricate		
[tʃ]	as in	chip, catch	[dʒ]	as in	judge, George, courageous

Approximants (all voiced)

[l]	as in	leap	[r] as in rip
[w]	as in	win	[j] as in yes

Vowels (note that the vowels are all voiced approximants)

RP	SSE						RP	SSE		
[i]	[i]	as in	meet				[u]	[u]	as in	pool
[ɪ]	[ɪ]	as in	bit				[ʊ]	[u]	as in	pull
[eɪ]	[e]	as in	bait	[ə]	as in	hammer	[əʊ]	[o]	as in	boat
[ɛ]	[ɛ]	as in	bet	[ɜ]	as in	bird (Engl.)	[ʌ]	[ʌ]	as in	cut
							[ɒ]	[ɔ]		cot
							[ɔ]	[ɔ]		caught
[a]	[a]	as in	cat				[ɑ]	[a]	as in	father

vii

Diphthongs

RP	SSE	
[aɪ]	[ʌi]	as in time
[aʊ]	[ʌu]	as in house
[ɔɪ]	[ɔe]	as in boy
[ɪə]	[ɪə]	as in idea, fear

(Also [eɪ] as in bait and [əʊ] as in boat for RP speakers)

PREFACE

As the title suggests, this book is one of a series which aims to help you prepare for university. You may still be at the stage of deciding on which courses to choose and, if you are not lucky enough to be at a school which teaches English Language, you may be wondering what the subject consists of. This book will give you a clear idea of the kind of topics covered. Even if you are already studying English Language at school, this book will help you to acquire the skills you need to carry out project work and will suggest some ways of thinking and some questions to ask about language. If you work your way through the book over the summer holidays, you will get off to a flying start in your university career and, for first-year university students, if you feel you have missed some of the basics or if you are struggling with any part of your course, this book will help you to consolidate your knowledge and get you going in the right direction.

There is no glossary, but the page numbers in bold type in the index will direct you to the place in the text where you can find a definition and examples of any linguistic term.

Before, and while I was writing the book, I consulted a large number of students and asked them what advice and help they would pass on to anyone starting English Language at university. The most frequent response was 'learn some grammar'. You really need to know the parts of speech if you are going to keep up with and understand the rest of the course. That is why there are rather more exercises in the syntax chapter than elsewhere in the book. The second most common response was 'I didn't have a clue how to write an English Language essay'. I am very grateful to Alexa Wilkinson for giving me her permission to use her first-year essay as an example.

Other comments from students include:

- I thought I was going to hate it, but I really like it now.

- I like it because it's all very rational.

- It's not as difficult as it looks – stick with it.

- It's very different from my other subjects, so it makes a nice change.

- I wish I'd just got on and learned the phonetic symbols right at the start.

Students have been very helpful in giving me feedback as the book was being written. They tested various chapters when they were finding their coursework hard or had identified gaps in their knowledge. They all said they wished they had had a book like this to get them started.

English Language is a wide-ranging subject and there should be something in it to appeal to most tastes and, even if you do not choose to study it for its own sake, you will find that it complements a number of other subjects including Linguistics, Literature, Philosophy and Theatre or Media Studies. If you are studying a foreign language, it makes a lot of sense to learn a bit more about your own. Even sociologists, lawyers and computer scientists can learn something from English Language.

I have tried to say a little about most of the commonly taught English Language topics. You may not meet all of these in your first year. Take a look at your own syllabus to see which areas to concentrate on. I have covered the 'tools' topics first and the 'applied' topics, where you will see the tools being used, later in the book. You may find the early chapters a little daunting; English Language is intellectually challenging and I did not want to give any false impression that it might be an easy option. Remember, when you get to university, you will not be trying to do it on your own. You will have the support of lecturers, tutors and other students. The section on Study Skills will give you some hints as to how to get the most out of the teaching and the facilities available. After a year of study, the essay and the exam in the appendices will be well within your abilities, and whether you choose to specialise in English Language, or whether you only study it for one year, I'm sure you will find it both useful and enjoyable.

INTRODUCTION

WHY GO TO UNIVERSITY?

You may be a seeker after knowledge, or you may be going for the social life, or you may be going because it is expected of you. Whatever your reasons, graduation day comes and you have to find a job. You would expect a university degree to improve your job prospects, but have you ever wondered why? Unless you become a teacher, the chances of English Language becoming the main focus of your employment are remote. Even with a general arts degree, the market for professional philosophers and literary critics is very limited. What employers are actually looking for are transferable skills and you have to make sure your prospective employer knows you have them.

General transferable skills

- University graduates are self-motivating.

- They are good at time management.

- They can work under pressure.

- They can meet deadlines.

- They have learned from their tutorials how to be team players and how to work as part of a group.

- They have shown that they are well-rounded individuals by taking an active part in at least one of the sporting, social or intellectual activities offered by university societies or clubs.

WHY CHOOSE ENGLISH LANGUAGE?

Some of us study English Language for its own sake, finding it endlessly satisfying as an intellectual challenge or as window on life and literature. Others do it because it complements other courses: Literature, Modern Languages, Linguistics, Philosophy or History, for example. A few do it because they have to. Of these, some make a point of loathing it on principle, but the majority find themselves enjoying it. The best reason for doing English Language is because you like it, but it brings its own transferable skills bonuses which often go unrecognised and which will be of lifelong service to you.

English Language transferable skills

When you reach the giddy heights of final year and start looking around for a career, you might like to point out to a prospective employer how your study of English Language, whether you did it at Honours, or whether you only did it for a year, has made you the very person for the job.

- English Language enhances your written communication skills. You will know how to write clearly, concisely and, above all, accurately and unambiguously. You will also be adept at matching the level of formality to suit different types of readers.

- English Language enhances your reading skills. You will be able to analyse non-literary texts and make sense of the most difficult constructions. You will even be able to spot when and why a very wise-sounding text may make no sense at all. You will read between the lines.

- English Language enhances your oral and aural skills. You will have confidence in your own accent. You will not prejudge people because their accents are different from yours. You will understand how accommodation and turntaking work in conversations and people will find you easy to talk to.

- Perhaps the greatest advantage that English Language brings is the enhancement of your thinking skills. Few subjects bring together the many different ways of thinking that English Language demands. You need to think clearly, methodically and logically. You will be able to seek out and evaluate evidence. Because you will be able to detect wooliness in language, you will instantly detect wooliness in the thinking behind it. You will also have creativity and flair. Not only will you have bright ideas but, additionally, you will be able to analyse them and explain how they work.

What employer could resist?

A SPECIAL WORD TO MATURE STUDENTS

Some mature students worry too much. If you are a mature student coming to university for the first time, you may have many problems to contend with that students straight from school do not have. You may have family commitments, perhaps even young children and all the worries about child-care that parenthood entails. Your university may provide good quality, low-cost childcare. This is worth finding out about. You may have got out of the habit of studying, writing essays and sitting exams and the young students may seem incredibly self-confident and knowledgeable. You will soon get back into the way of studying and you would not have been admitted to university if you did not have the ability to succeed; so there is no reason to compare your talents un-favourably with those of younger students. For some reason, many mature students feel that they have to do better than the younger students to prove to themselves that they can do as well. If this sounds like you, calm down. Your maturity gives you extra skills, particularly in time management and com-munication. It is always a joy to teach mature students because of their high level of motivation and because they ask lots of questions. If any domestic crises should occur, or if you are having difficulty with any aspect of study, you will find that members of staff are very understanding and supportive.

PART I
What is English Language?

1 PHONETICS AND PHONOLOGY: THE SOUNDS OF ENGLISH

Learning outcomes

- to be conscious of language as spoken rather than written

- to appreciate that a language is a system of sounds

- to be able to identify and describe the phonemes of English

- to be able to hear and describe some allophones

- to be ready for later chapters such as Regional Variation

Phonetics is the study of speech sounds, how they are made, how they are transmitted and how they are heard. Phonology is the study of the sound system of a particular language. An English Language course deals with phonetics in a different way from a Linguistics course because it focuses on the sounds which are relevant to English. Phonetics and phonology are of immense practical value. Without them, the more applied areas of English Language, such as dialectology or the history of English, would be impossible to study and they have a valuable contribution to make to many professions including speech therapy, foreign language teaching, primary school teaching and acting.

These are not the easiest subjects to learn from a book because they involve sound. They also involve learning new skills, and skills have to be practised. At university, you will have the opportunity to practise with a teacher and the sounds, symbols and terminology will quickly become familiar.

We spend so much of our academic life dealing with the written word that we often forget that language is, first and foremost, spoken. It is the task of the phonologist to study the system of speech sounds of a language. Of all the many thousands of sounds that we can utter, only a small number are actually used to form words. The smallest units of sound which we use to distinguish between one word and another are known as **phonemes**. *Nip* sounds different from *sip*. It is the difference between the two initial sounds that tells us we are dealing with two different words. So the *n* and the *s* must represent two different phonemes. Similarly *nip* differs by a single sound from *nap*. Again, this tells us we are hearing two different phonemes. You can go on finding contrasting pairs of words until you have isolated all the phonemes that are needed to make English words.

These phonemes are the sounds that your ears have been 'tuned into' from a very early age, even before you were born. As a baby, you began to sort out the sounds which are important for your own language and to disregard the sounds which don't help to distinguish English words. This is why children who suffer from conditions like glue-ear, which produce spells of deafness in their early years, can have problems with their speech and sometimes later on with their spelling. Also, because your ear learns to hear these sounds, it can reconstruct them from the distorted and incomplete speech and background crackle that come to you down a telephone line. If you do not have all the phonemes of a language from childhood, it is very hard to acquire them later. Have you ever tried to teach a French person to say *ship*? Not only do they keep saying *sheep* but they find it very difficult, if not impossible, even to hear the difference between *ship* and *sheep*, far less reproduce it. This is because the vowel phoneme in *ship* is not one of the French list of phonemes and French ears will simply hear it as the nearest phoneme in their own language. So it sounds to the learner as if you are saying, 'not *sheep* but *sheep*'. No wonder he or she finds it hard! You will have similar problems learning a foreign language when you come across a phoneme which is new to you. Phonology provides essential insights for the teaching of English as a foreign language and it is easier to learn a foreign language when you know how your own language works.

Even in English, when we look at different periods and different accents, we find that the list of phonemes may be slightly altered. For example, the sound that the Scots use at the end of *loch* has been lost from southern Standard English. For most Scots *pool* and *pull* sound the same, although they sound different to English or American speakers. Phonology is also concerned with the rules for putting sounds together and how these rules change: the spelling of words like *knife* and *gnash* indicate that words could, at an earlier stage in the history of the language, start with combinations of consonants which no longer appear in initial position. So an understanding of phonology is essential in order to study language change and variation, historical and modern, social and regional.

So far as English is concerned, writing is an attempt to represent the spoken word on a page by means of a series of symbols, or letters, each one originally intended to represent a sound, but spelling has not kept pace with changes in the spoken language. As a result, our spelling system is now too confusing to be much use for describing sounds: some of the letters of the alphabet can be used for more than one sound like the letter <c> in *circus, school, science*; some sounds can be spelt in more than one way as in *kick, Rikki, Raquel, cat,* or *I, eye, ay, tie, spy, time, tight*; some sounds have no one letter to represent them and then pairs of letters have to be invented like <sh> as in *sheep* or <ch> as in *chip* (and what about *Christmas* or *chiropodist* or the Scots pronunciation of *loch*?). How many people realise that <th> has two pronunciations, one as in *thy* and the other as in *thigh*? To complicate things further, we have the now 'silent' letters in *knee, gnash, comb* and strange irregularities like *bough* and *cough*.

You will notice that spelling letters are enclosed in pointed brackets < > to distinguish them from sounds which go in square brackets [ ]. Try to master the different brackets – you will find them increasingly useful.

Clearly, if we are going to write about sounds, we need a

more reliable method than the ordinary alphabet and this is why we use the **International Phonetic Alphabet** (IPA). This, as its name suggests, is internationally recognised and allows us to describe any language in an unambiguous way. You will find it used as a guide to pronunciation in most good dictionaries. It can be used it to represent very subtle details of pronunciation and different regional accents can be transcribed with great accuracy, but this requires familiarity with many symbols and a lot of practice. A less detailed knowledge of the IPA is expected of first-year students but even this is immensely useful. Many of the symbols are obvious, like [p], [t], [k], [m] and [n]. Occasionally, because it is used internationally, one or two of the symbols relate to other languages better than they do to English. For example, the sound that we usually spell with a <y> as in *yes, yet, yellow* (but not in *spy*) is represented by [j]. There are very few of these awkward ones, though, and unfamiliar symbols used in this book will be accompanied by an example word. The important thing to remember in phonology is to forget spelling and listen to what you actually say.

SPEECH SOUNDS

Speech is composed of **consonants** and **vowels**. What are they and how do we articulate or physically produce these sounds? You can think of the organs of speech as if they were part of a wind instrument. The air from the lungs is acted upon by various parts of the **vocal tract** to change the sound it makes when it reaches the outside world.

CONSONANTS

Consonants are easy to describe because they involve a definite obstruction in the vocal tract. Make a [p] sound, and now a [b]. You will notice that you close your lips completely and this acts as a barrier to the breath. Such consonants are knows as **stops**. Some stops, like [p] and [b] are released with a kind of mini-explosion and so these stops are known as **plosive** consonants. Now try [s] and [z]. The tongue is close to the roof of the mouth so that the channel for the breath is restricted and you hear friction. Therefore, these are known as **fricatives**. In sounds like [w], the obstruction is not enough to make friction and the breath can flow more freely. These sounds are known as **approximants**. So in describing consonants, we look at the **manner** of making the obstruction.

Obviously, [p] and [t] are made in different parts of the mouth. So the **place** of articulation is important.

Then, as we have heard, [s] and [z] are both fricatives. They are both made in the same place, just behind the teeth. What is the difference between them? The answer is **voicing**. In other words, [s] is made with the breath only, but for [z] the vocal cords vibrate like the reed of a woodwind instrument.

When defining consonants, the most important things to learn, and listen for, are **voicing, place** and **manner**.

1. Voicing

Is the sound made with breath only or breath + voice? In other words, is it voiceless or voiced? You can feel this by putting your fingers on the front of your throat and making a [s] then [z]. Can you feel the difference? What you feel with [z] is vibration from the vocal cords. You can hear the difference by saying [s] and [z] with your hands over your ears. You can sing the difference. Try singing a scale using [z]. Try it with [s]. What happens?

Note how many of the consonants can be regarded as voiced/voiceless pairs, like [b] and [p] or [v] and [f]. Now we are able to describe the difference between the two sounds which share the spelling <th>. The initial sound is all that distinguishes between *thy* and *thigh*. *Thy* has a voiced sound represented in the IPA by the symbol [ð] and *thigh* has the voiceless sound represented a *th*eta [θ].

The voiceless consonants are [p], [t], [k], [f], [θ] as in *thigh*, [s], [ʃ] as in *she*, [h] and [tʃ] as in *chew*.

The voiced consonants are [b], [d], [g], [v], [ð] as in *thy*, [z], [ʒ] as in *rouge*, [r], [l], [j] as in *yes*, [dʒ] *judge*, [w], [m], [n] and [ŋ] as in *sing*.

2. Place

Where does the obstruction occur and which articulators are involved?

a) **Bilabial**: Both lips [p], [b], [m], [w] *witch*.
b) **Labio-dental**: Upper teeth and lower lip [f], [v].
c) **Dental**: Tongue and teeth [θ] *thigh*, [ð] *thy*.
d) **Alveolar**: Tongue and alveolar ridge (gum ridge which you can feel behind your upper teeth before the palate arches upwards) [t], [d], [n], [l], [s], [z].
e) **Post-alveolar**: Tongue curls back behind alveolar ridge as [r].
f) **Palato-alveolar**: Tongue and back of alveolar ridge/front of hard palate [ʃ] *show*, [ʒ] *rouge*, [tʃ] *chip*, [dʒ] *jump*.
g) **Palatal**: Centre of tongue and hard palate [j] *yes, yellow*.
h) **Velar**: Back of tongue and soft palate (velum) [k], [g], [ŋ], [w].
i) **Glottal**: The glottis is the opening to the larynx or 'voice box'. It takes a lot of practice to feel what is going on so far back. When you say [h] in isolation, you may be able to feel that it is glottal.

Note: If you are not sure where a sound is being articulated, say the sound and, without changing the position of the mouth, suck air in. You will feel cold where the articulators are closest together.

3. Manner

a) **Stops:** Two speech organs come together firmly, blocking the flow of air. Pressure builds up behind this closure so that an 'explosion' is heard when the organs part, hence the alternative name **plosives**: [p], [t], [k], [b], [d], [g]. **Nasal consonants** do not have the plosive release but they are still classified as stops. If you say [m], [n] or [ŋ] as in *sing* and hold your nose, you will feel a blockage, or stop, in the mouth. Normally, in making these nasal sounds, the velum or soft palate is lowered to let air escape through the nose. There are only three nasal sounds in English. All other sounds are classifies as **oral**.

b) **Fricatives:** Friction is heard where two speech organs come close together, making a very narrow passage for the outgoing breath. [f], [v], [θ] *thin,* [ð] *then,* [s], [z], [ʃ] *ash,* [ʒ] *leisure,* [h].

d) **Affricates:** These begin in the same way as a stop with firm contact between the two speech organs, but the release is gradual, creating friction [tʃ] *church,* [dʒ] *judge*.

e) **Approximants:** These are made by 'approximating' two organs or bringing them closer together but not close enough to cause friction [w], [j] *yes* and [r]. [l] is also an approximant but it is unique in English in that it is a lateral.

All the sounds of English are have a **central** airflow except the **lateral** consonant [l] where the airflow is round the sides of the tongue. You can verify this by saying [l] while sucking air inwards and feeling the sides of tongue grow cold.

VOWELS

Vowels are more difficult to describe because there is not the definite obstruction that you can feel in consonants. They are also where there is the greatest variation between accents, so do not be surprised if you do not recognise the vowels listed below. They are based on Received Pronunciation, the regionally neutral accent associated with speakers of Standard English in England. If you are Scots, you will probably not hear any difference between *pool* and *pull, caught* and *cot, psalm* and *Sam.* English speakers distinguish between these pairs of words and this means that they have three phonemes which most Scots do not have. Speakers from the north of England may not hear a difference between *look* and *luck,* because they lack a phoneme. Scottish speakers will find their accent discussed more fully in Chapter 6.

The vowels are shaped by the lips and the tongue.

Lips

The lips may be **rounded, relaxed** or **spread**. Compare *who* and *he*. For *who* they will be tightly rounded, but for *he* they may be spread. Now try the words *loo, low, law, lah* and you'll feel your lips move gradually from the rounded position to neutral or relaxed. By whispering the vowels and missing out the consonants, you can enhance the sensation. Now try keeping your lips rounded or spread all the time – even when not appropriate – and notice how your voice alters because you are changing the shape of your mouth.

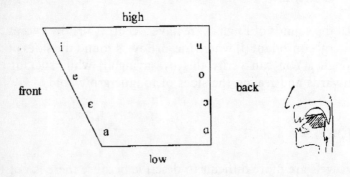

Figure 1.1   The vowel trapesium: putting some vowels on a map of the mouth

Height

For the moment, forget about what your lips are doing and compare *ha, he, who* keeping the tongue tip behind the lower teeth:

ha The jaw is lowered and there is a big gap between the tongue and the roof of the mouth. This is an **open** or **low** vowel.

he, who The jaw is raised and the tongue is much closer to the roof of the mouth. These are **close** or **high** vowels.

Back, Front or Central

Now whisper through the sequence *ha, hay, he,* again with the tongue anchored behind the lower teeth. You will feel the tongue rise up and forward.

When describing a vowel as **front** or **back** we are referring to the highest point of the tongue. Try saying *oooo~eeee~oooo~eeee* and try to feel the backness and frontness. With *eeee,* or [i], if you keep the tip of your tongue behind your teeth, you will feel your tongue humped up towards the front of your hard palate. With *oooo,* or [u], the hump in your tongue is much further back. Freeze your mouth in the [i] and [u] positions and then suck in air as hard as you can until you can feel your mouth grow cold where the narrowing is. You should feel that [i] is front and [u] is back.

A vowel symbol which you will find very frequently in transcriptions is [ə]. This symbol is called *schwa* and it represents the indeterminate vowel that you find in unstressed syllables. It is neither back, front, high or low but somewhere in the middle. If you have ever wondered whether a word was spelt *-ible* or *-able*, this is because what you really say is [əbl].

DIPHTHONGS

These involve the tongue moving from one position to another so that you start off at one vowel and finish at another. Scottish and English speakers both have diphthongs in *time*, *house* and *boy*. They are [aɪ], [aʊ], and [ɔɪ] if you are English, or [ʌi], [ʌu] and [ɔe] if you are Scottish. There is another diphthong for Scottish speakers which occurs in words like *idea* and, additionally for English speakers, in *fear*, *beer* etc. This is the [ɪə] diphthong.

English speakers have diphthongs in words like *bait* [eɪ] and *boat* [əʊ] where Scottish speakers simply have [e] and [o].

PHONEMES AND THEIR BRACKETS

The phoneme was defined above as the smallest unit of sound which could make the difference between two words. Scottish and English speakers would agree that they are both saying the word *boat*, whether they say [bot] or [bəʊt]. A Scottish speaker in an informal situation would very probably end the word with a glottal stop [boʔ] not making contact with the alveolar ridge as you would expect for a [t] sound. But, again, the word itself does not change. A single phoneme can change its actual pronunciation depending on the regional accent of the speaker, the formality of the situation, the surrounding phonemes or even on whether or not the speaker has a cold or a mouthful of chewing gum. The phoneme is really a theoretical generalisation. To distinguish the phoneme from a real sound that a real speaker makes on a real occasion, slanting brackets // are used. So, the <oa> and <t> spellings in *boat* represent the /o/ phoneme and the /t/ phoneme and some speakers will pronounce /bot/ as [bəʊt] and other speakers will pronounce it as [boʔ]. (The choice of /o/ for the name of the phoneme is arbitrary. Some other books choose to call it /əʊ/. What matters is that we all know we are talking about the sound that distinguishes *boot* from *boat*, irrespective of the finer points of pronunciation.)

Another example shows how the surrounding sounds can affect the pronunciation of a phoneme. Consider the /n/ phoneme in the word *ten*. Is it the same phoneme as in the word *tenth*? Yes, of course it is. However, if you feel what your tongue does with these two /n/ phonemes, you will find a subtle difference. When you say *ten*, /tɛn/, the /n/ phoneme is pronounced, as expected, as an alveolar nasal stop [tɛn]. When you say *tenth*, /tɛnθ/, the /n/ phoneme has the tongue further forward, on the teeth, anticipating the dental fricative [tɛn̪θ]. (The little 'tooth' indicates a dental pronunciation.) Say *ten* with this dental pronunciation. Does it turn *ten* into a different word? No. Most people would not even notice the difference. Ears and brains are not programmed to listen for it: they selectively pick out and interpret phonemes and ignore variations on phonemes.

The importance of distinguishing between phonemes and their actual realisations (**allophones**) will become clearer in the chapters dealing with the practical topics of language change and variation (Chapters 7–9).

PRE-UNIVERSITY CHALLENGE

Here are a few words you might like to try transcribing in the IPA. They get harder as they go along. You are going to transcribe what you actually say and therefore you should use square brackets. Be careful!

Tin ship him hymn ham lamb knee chip catch
click plough pig ping pink think that grudge yes
cats queens kisses

Answers

[tɪn]	An easy one to start with.
[ʃɪp]	One sound, one symbol. Neat.
[hɪm]	How easy can this get?
[hɪm]	This sounds the same as the last one.

[ham]   Yes, it's another easy one.
[lam]   Did the final letter in the spelling catch you out?
[ni]   If you don't say it, you don't transcribe it.
[tʃɪp]
[katʃ]   No, there isn't one.
[klɪk]
[plaʊ]   Easy if you just listen to what you say.
[pɪg]
[pɪŋ]   Note there are only three sounds.
[pɪŋk]   Did you notice how you get [ŋ] in anticipation of the
           following velar?
[θɪŋk]   The voiceless one.
[ðat]   The voiced one.
[grʌdʒ]
[jɛs]
[kats]   Look at that plural. Why is it different from the next
           one?
[kwinz]   Who needs *qu*? Is [n] voiced or voiceless?
[kɪsɪz]   Here is another way of marking the plural. Why is
           the final sound voiced? (See p. 31)

To English readers:

[aɪ ɪkspɛkt ju faʊnd ðɪs kwaɪt streɪtfɔwəd ənd aɪ həʊp jul
ɛndʒɔɪ duɪŋ ɛksəsaɪzɪz laɪk ðɪs ət jʊnɪvɜsɪti]

To Scottish readers:

[ʌi ɪkspɛkt ju fʌund ðɪs kwʌit stretfɔrwʌrd ənd ʌi hop jul
ɛndʒɔe duɪŋ ɛksʌrsʌɪzɪz lʌɪk ðɪs ət junɪvɛrsɪte]

FURTHER READING

Giegerich, H. (1992) *English Phonology: An introduction*, Cambridge: Cambridge
University Press. The best text to use in conjunction with this book.

Ladefoged, P. (1993) *A Course in Phonetics*, London: Harcourt Brace College. More of a work book. Some user-friendly exercises.

McMahon, A. (2002) *An Introduction to English Phonology*, Edinburgh: Edinburgh University Press. A very approachable textbook, ideal for first year.

Ignore spelling and listen to what you really say.

Consonants: place, manner, voiced/voiceless, oral/nasal

Vowels: front, back, high, low

Buzz words: phoneme, allophone

2 VOCABULARY

Learning outcomes

- to think about the relationship between words and the real world

- to know where words come from

- to be able to analyse the internal structure of words

There are many different ways in which to discuss words. Semantics and the formation of new words are the mostly likely aspects to be covered in a first-year course. This chapter takes a brief look at semantics and concentrates on word formation, reluctantly omitting other aspects such as lexicography.

SEMANTICS

Semantics is the study of meaning, or how words relate to the real world, grouping words into semantic fields (related by subject) and arranging them in hierarchies within semantic fields (carrots, peas and beans can all be grouped as vegetables; vegetables, meats and dairy products can all be grouped as food). Semantics is concerned with sense relationships such as synonymy, antonymy and hyponymy. **Synonymy** refers to words with similar meaning like *determined*, *stubborn* and *pig-headed* or *regal*, *royal* and *kingly*. Although words in each of these two sets express similar meanings, they are not exactly interchangeable. Not just meaning, but also formality level and even point of view will determine which word is chosen on any particular occasion. Do you think there are any exact synonyms in English? **Antonymy** is concerned with opposites like *good* and *bad*, *long* and *short*. **Hyponymy** has to do with the relationship where one thing is an example of a kind. *Dogs*, *cats* and *horses* are all *animals*. *Silver*, *copper* and *iron* are all *metals*. The examples are **hyponyms** and the category name is the **hypernym**. Also within the remit of semantics is the study of **collocations**, or which words occur together. *Will* and *testament* or *fish* and *chips* are frequent collocations. There are some words which cannot occur together. You can talk about *a powerful man*; you can talk about a *strong man*; you can talk about *a powerful car*; but can you say 'a strong car'? *Strong* is not found in collocation with *car*.

We could study vocabulary as etymologists, discovering where words and their meanings come from, sometimes tracing them back through many changes to ancient origins. The vocabulary (or lexicon) of English is changing all the time. Some old words change their meaning or die out and new ones come into use. The chapters on the history of English and language change (Chapters 5 and 9) will address changes in the lexicon and the origins of older loan words. This chapter now goes on to focus on word formation, or the formation of new **lexical items**, in Present Day English (PDE).

(The expression 'lexical item' may seem like a rather long-winded way of saying 'word', but what is a word? Is *cat* the same 'word' as *cats*? Is *compact disk* one 'word' or two? *Cat* and *cats* are the same lexical item and *compact disk* is a single lexical item, as are *wash up* and *get on*. The technical term allows us to be more precise and unambiguous.)

In grammatical word formation, there is an order in which things are done; there are relationships to be analysed; there are sets of rules which can be seen in action The non-grammatical means of word formation, on the other hand, are not systematic in any way. There are no rules. Each new word produced by these methods comes into the language as an individual, randomly. We start off with some of the more productive methods of non-grammatical word formation.

NON-GRAMMATICAL WORD FORMATION

Loans

English has been borrowing words from other languages for a very long time. Although OE tended to avoid borrowing if it could make up new words from its existing word stock, Old Scandinavian words were borrowed into Northern Old English when the Danish Vikings settled in Yorkshire and the surrounding area (*law*, *skin*); the followers of William the Conqueror brought Norman French words with them (*mutton*, *prison*). Since the Middle Ages, we have been borrowing from Latin (*regal*) and Central French (*royal*). The Renaissance saw a massive influx of loans from Latin, Greek, Italian and other languages and we have been borrowing unashamedly ever since. We go on holiday, or just as far as the shopping centre, and come back with *pizzas*, *baguettes*, *paella* and *frankfurters*. We open the newspapers and read about a *coup d'état* or *glasnost*. Borrowing is a very productive way of expanding the lexicon. What languages do you think the following words came from?

pyjamas, potato, powwow, opera, kohl, cola

You can find out from any good dictionary.

Eponyms

Eponyms are words taken from proper names. They may be taken from personal names: *sandwich* (after the Earl of Sandwich who pioneered the packed lunch), *biro* (after the inventor of the ball-point pen), *mackintosh* (after the man who rubberised cloth to make it waterproof). Eponyms can also be formed from placenames as in *denim* (de Nîmes), *jodhpurs* and *balaclava*. Even trade names can eventually become part of the language: many people are more likely to say *hoovering* than 'vacuum-cleaning'.

An important thing to note about eponyms is the loss of the initial capital letter. This signals a move away from proper name status to ordinary word status.

Acronyms

This is a particularly popular method of word formation in modern times. An acronym is formed from the initial letters of a phrase and pronounced as if these letters spelt a word. Sometimes the word is written in lower case letters throughout, like *ecu* (European Currency Unit), even although there were capitals in the original phrase. Sometimes an initial capital survives as in *Aids* (Acquired Immune Deficiency Syndrome). There may even be capitals throughout as in *NATO* (North Atlantic Treaty Organisation). Occasionally, a bit of licence is allowed as in *Radar* (Radio Detection and Ranging).

Acronyms should be distinguished from abbreviations, in which the initial letters are spelt out: *BBC, DJ, GP, MA*. Occasionally there are examples which can be pronounced either way: *VAT* can either be spelt out or pronounced [vat]. There are even hybrids like *CD-ROM*.

Clippings

When words are shortened, they are referred to as clippings. The end of the word may be removed to form a back-clipping like *piano* (from pianoforte), *fan* (from fanatic) or *porn* (from pornography). Conversely, a front-clipping has the start of the word removed: *phone* (telephone), *bus* (omnibus). There are also front-and-back-clippings like *fridge* (refrigerator) and *car* (motor carriage). Compound clippings include *sci-fi* (science fiction).

This method of word production has become more frequent in recent years but it is not entirely new. The Victorians invented the word *bumf*, a useful word nowadays when computers generate vast quantities of unnecessary and unwanted printout. At least we know the Victorians put their scrap paper to practical use; *bumf* is their back-clipping from bumfodder, a word which has been in use since the seventeenth century.

Blends

There is a group of words which can be seen as a special kind of compound clipping. These consist of a back-clipping and a front-clipping joined together: *mo*(tor ho)*tel*, *fan*(atic maga)-*zine*, *br*(eakfast l)*unch*.

Rhyming slang

Usually associated with Cockney dialect, rhyming slang consists of two or three words, the last of which rhymes with the word for which the rhyming slang word is substituted. So *apples and pears* means 'stairs'. Rhyming slang is not exclusive to Cockney, though. The Scots example *corned beef* demonstrates this because it only rhymes with the Scots pronunciation of *deaf* [dif] and not with the English pronunciation [dɛf]. To make rhyming slang even more obscure, the rhyming word is often omitted: *china* means 'mate' (china plate).

Onomatopoeia

The sound of onomatopoeic words is supposed to be like their meaning. *Crash! Bang! Tinkle!*

Metaphor

Many words that were first used in a metaphorical way have taken on a life of their own and are now longer seen as metaphors, until you stop and think about it. *Crown* can mean a false tooth, the top of the head, a coin or a clump of plant roots. The *golden rule* is to never to take a word *lightly* at its *face* value but to *dig* into *key* changes in its history. Do you get the *point*? Often, metaphors are used to create euphemisms.

Euphemisms

There are some things we do not like to talk about. *Water closet* or *WC* started off as a euphemism, but we all know what really goes on in the WC and so the word outwore its function as a euphemism and *lavatory* was adopted instead. The original meaning of the word lavatory was 'a place to wash'. That word, in turn, became embarrassing to some people who go on looking for new, increasingly silly, euphemisms to avoid saying what they mean: *powder-room, restroom, comfort-station.*

Made-up words

Apart from nonsense words, neologisms which are purely made up are surprisingly hard to find. *Scag* and *quark* are probably made up.

Getting it together

There are words which have undergone a number of processes before reaching their present form. Think for a moment about the word *veggieburger*. You will recognise a back-clipping of *vegetable*, or perhaps *vegetarian*, a word formed by affixation,

as described below. The rest of the word obviously comes
from *hamburger*, a loan word from German, but formed in
German as an eponym from the placename *Hamburg* plus a
suffix. Once we got the word *hamburger* into English, we
totally disregarded its true etymology and, in spite of the fact
that we know a hamburger is not made from ham, we
substituted what we perceive as one ingredient for another,
spawning a whole menu of *beefburgers, cheeseburgers, chick-
enburgers* and *veggieburgers*. Mr Thomas Crapper who invented the flush toilet underwent eponymy and back-clipping.
See if you can deduce or track down the origins of *caravan,
squiggle, deli, badminton, algebra, piano, the Sweeney, sofa.*

GRAMMATICAL WORD FORMATION
(DERIVATIONAL MORPHOLOGY)

In Chapter 1, we looked at phonemes, the smallest units of
sound which may be used to distinguish between two words.
These phonemes, however, have no meaning in themselves. It
is only when they are grouped together into recognisable
words or recognisable bits of words that meaning starts to
appear. Prefixes like *un-* or *non-* carry a sense of negativity.
Suffixes often tell you about a part of speech: *-ness* (as in
goodness) tells you that you are looking at a noun; *-ous, -ful* or
-less tell you that you are looking at an adjective (*glorious,
plentiful, hopeless*); *-ly* usually suggests an adverb (*quickly*).
Some suffixes do not change the part of speech, for example
the diminutive suffixes *-ette* (*cigarette)* and *-ock* (*hillock*)
attach to nouns and these remain nouns. (For an explanation
of the parts of speech, see Chapter 4.)

These building-brick bits of words are known as **morphemes,** and **derivational morphology** is the study of how
the morphemes can be combined by **affixation** and **compounding** to create new words or **lexical items** which can
be added to the dictionary. Brace brackets { } are used to
enclose morphemes.

Roots

The first type of morpheme to consider is the **root**. This is the core of a word which cannot be stripped down any further. For example, *unhelpfully* is built up around the root {help}. In this instance, the root happens to be a lexical item in its own right. It can exist as a complete entity without any prefixes or suffixes. Such a root is known as a **free root morpheme**. Other roots can only be found attached to other morphemes. These roots are referred to as **bound root morphemes**. For example {dent-} is a root because we can add the suffixes {-al} and {-ist}, but it does not exist on its own and so it must be a bound root morpheme.

Compounding

Two or more roots can be joined to form a compound. Usually, the meaning of the compound is not quite the same in meaning as the sum of its parts. A *blackbird* is rather more specific than a *black bird*. A *greengrocer* is not from Mars. You will also note that many compounds, including these two examples, undergo a change of stress which underlines that fact that the two roots have become a single word.

Compounds can be made up of various parts of speech. Adjective + noun (*greenfly*), or noun + noun (*eggcup*) are very common. What other combinations can you think of? How are the words related to each other? Is there a headword? A *greenfly* is a fly and a *motorbike* is a bike. *User-friendly* is friendly. Curiously, some compounds do not contain a headword like this. If you looked at the parts of such a compound, you could not guess what the word related to. For example, *redhead* is neither red nor a head, but a person who has red hair. The headword (the unstated person) is outside the word itself and that kind of compound is called **exocentric**. Other examples of exocentric compounds are *pickpocket* and *greybeard*. They are not a very common kind of compound. Compounds are much more likely to be **endocentric** with the headword as one of its parts.

Affixation

Affixation is concerned with making new lexical items by adding prefixes and suffixes in a systematic, rule-governed way. It is because affixation is rule-governed that we describe it as a grammatical method of word formation. Affixes may be described as class-maintaining or class-changing, depending on whether they change the part of speech. The bit of a word that the prefix or suffix is added to is called a base. So the root {help} is also a base to which {-ful} is added and {helpful} then becomes the base to which {un-} is added and so on until the final lexical item *unhelpfully* is complete. Prefixes and suffixes are bound morphemes.

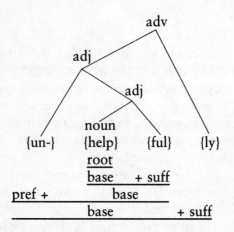

- {un-} bound negative prefix (class-maintaining)

- {help} free root

- {-ful} bound adjective-forming suffix (class-changing)

- {-ly} bound adverb-forming suffix (class-changing)

One of the ways in which derivational morphology is rule-governed is that you cannot just add any old prefix anywhere and there is an order in which they must be added. Usually, the order is obvious: you could not add {un-} to {help} until you have added {-ful}. At other times, it is not so clear. In what order would you attach these morphemes?

{un-}   {happy}   {-nes}

This is a rule-governed process and so we must look for a rule. With *unhappiness* we could say that there were two possible rules for the affixation of {un-}:

1. {un-} + adj > adj (if we say {un-} attaches to {happy} first)

or

2. {un-} + noun > noun (if we form {happiness} first)

Which rule is better? Looking back to *unhelpful*, we can see that {un-} + noun was not permissible. Therefore {un-} + adj is the better rule because it applies in more cases. Can you decide what the rule would be for the negative prefix {in-} by considering the morphemes {in-} {sense} {-ible} and {in-} {sane} {-ity}?

Allomorphy

A root or an affix can take a slightly different form depending on the adjacent sounds. If we look at the negative prefix morpheme {in-}, we find it in *invisible, indestructible, incompetent* and so on, but we also find it in *impossible, imbalance, immature, illegal, illogical, irregular* and *irrefutable*. What has happened is that the /n/ phoneme anticipates the following sound. In the case of the bilabials /p/, /b/ and /m/, the /n/ itself becomes the bilabial nasal. Where {in-} is followed by /l/ or /r/, the assimilation is complete. When looking for allomorphy, you must disregard the spelling. There is no allomorphy involved in {happy} + {-ly}

because it is only the spelling and not the sound that changes, but in *sanity*

{sane} + {-ity}
/san/ + /ətɪ/

the root is the bound allomorph /san/ of the free root morpheme {sane} and the free allomorph which appears in the words *sane* and *sanely* is /sen/.

Conversion

This is simply when a word changes its part of speech without any affixation, as when the noun *party* becomes as verb: *Let's party all night*. This method of word formation is also called **functional shift** or **zero morpheme derivation**. Can you explain why this last name is particularly descriptive? Further examples include noun to verb conversions such as *to badger, to guarantee, to e-mail, to stage, to access, to text*; verb to noun conversions like *scratch, split, scan, jog*; and adjective to verb conversions like *to lower, to better* and *to numb*. There are also adjective to noun conversions: an environmentally concerned *green*; a right-wing true *blue*; c'mon you *reds*!

Things to think about

All sorts of complications have arisen because of borrowing from other languages when we have recognised foreign morphemes and made them productive in English word formation. In the early stages, native morphemes were kept together and foreign morphemes went together. So native {un-} usually goes with native roots to give *unhappy, untrue* etc., and {in-} goes with French or Latin loans *inconsolable, indubitable*. As these morphemes have become more naturalised, these barriers have broken down and we get mixtures like *unco-operative*. The eponym *marathon* has produced the totally spurious {-athon} suffix in *swimathon, kissathon* and so on.

Familiar affixes may be attached to roots of which the meaning is no longer familiar to many people. At what point does a morpheme cease to exist in its own right? If we lose the meaning, do we lose the morpheme? This is a bit of a grey area. In *cranberry*, we recognise {-berry} as the morpheme used in *elderberry, strawberry* and so on. but {cran-} no longer carries meaning as a bound allomorph of the free morpheme *crane*, although presumably it originated from the shape of the cranberry flower, resembling a crane's beak. It occurred in that single lexical item but has recently started to become productive with the new compound *cranapple*. Is *happy* a morphologically simple word or is it made up of the obsolete noun *hap*, with a narrowing in meaning from 'chance' to 'good chance' and the adjective forming suffix {-y}? Perhaps. However, most English speakers are not botanists, nor Latin scholars, nor historical linguists and derivational morphology in a first year English Language course usually describes the way in which we make new lexical items now.

Once a new lexical item has been formed by any of the above means, and added to the lexicon, we can then begin to use it in real sentences, and any further affixation that this requires is a matter of inflectional morphology, the subject of the next chapter.

Further reading

Bauer, L. (1983) *English Word Formation*, Cambridge: Cambridge University Press. This is an excellent, authoritative book for the serious student.

Carstairs-McCarthy, A. (2002) *An Introduction to English Morphology*, Edinburgh: Edinburgh University Press. The ideal introduction with inviting exercises and fully discussed answers.

Katamba, Francis (1993) *Morphology*, Basingstoke: Macmillan Press. This is a linguistics textbook which deals with morphology in many different languages but it is very approachable and stimulating. It contains plenty of exercises (without answers).

Non-grammatical word formation: loans, eponyms, acronyms, clippings, blends, rhyming slang, onomatopoeia, metaphor, euphemism

Grammatical word formation: affixation, compounding, conversion

Buzzwords: morpheme, allomorph, root, prefix, suffix, lexical item

3 INFLECTIONAL MORPHOLOGY

Learning outcome

● to recognise and describe how a word carries grammatical information

In the second part of Chapter 2, we combined morphemes to make new lexical items to put in the dictionary or lexicon. That is where derivational morphology stops. When you take a word out of the lexicon and put it in a sentence, you may have to alter the word in some way to make it work the right way in relation to that particular sentence. This is the province of **inflectional morphology**. We shall be dealing with the inflectional morphology of different parts of speech and, if the parts of speech or any other grammatical terms are not familiar to you, you might like to refer to Chapter 4.

DECLENSION CLASS WORDS

The declension class words are nouns, adjectives, determiners and pronouns. The inflections associated with declension class words show **number** (singular or plural) **person** and **case**. Not all declension class words show much in the way of inflectional morphology in Present Day English (PDE) and, since personal pronouns show more morphology than the others, we will start with them.

Pronouns

What is the difference between *I* and *we*, *he* and *they*, *her* and *them*? Obviously, one of each pair is singular and the other plural. In PDE, **number** is as easy as that.

Person can be first, second or third. *I, me, my, we, us, our* are first person. Second person pronouns are *you* and *your*. Third person pronouns are *he, she, it, him, her, his, its, they, them, their*.

Case refers to the role that the word plays in the sentence. Historically, the cases found in Old English (OE) were **nominative**, used for the subject of the sentence (*I need chocolate urgently.*), **accusative** used for the object of the sentence (*The aliens took me to their leader.*) and the **genitive** which usually expresses possession (*This is my sentence. This sentence is mine.*) In OE, the accusative was used, not only for the object, but also after some prepositions and other prepositions were followed by the **dative** (*Say it to me*). Of course, in Present Day English (PDE), the accusative and the dative have become indistinguishable and are often jointly referred to as the **oblique** case. You might like to look at the OE cases on page 67.

Can you give the case of the following pronouns?

his   them   our   she   your   him   its   us   we   you

You were probably doing well until you came to *you*. It could be either nominative or oblique. This is an example of **syncretism**, a process which has been going on since before Old English times. It involves a falling together of forms which once had different inflections but are now identical. *You* shows syncretism between the nominative and the oblique cases. In all the personal pronouns, there is syncretism between the accusative and the dative. In the relative pronouns, older speakers and Americans do still distinguish between the nominative *who* and the oblique *whom* but, for most British speakers, syncretism has occurred here too. As we shall see, syncretism is even more widespread in nouns and verbs. Inflectional morphology is getting easier all the time!

Nouns

If you look at the chapter on the history of English (Chapter 5), you will find all the forms of *the stone* listed. It is interesting to compare the OE morphology with PDE morphology. Not only will you see how much simpler PDE is but you will also see where the present forms come from.

PDE nouns show syncretism between the nominative and oblique cases. The only case that has a distinctive ending is the genitive. The genitive is marked by an -*s* which is conventionally represented as {-S}. In speech, for most nouns, you cannot tell a genitive singular from a plural of any case. This too is syncretism. In written language, it is only the convention of the apostrophe that allows us to distinguish the genitive singular and plural from the plural non-genitive: *This cat's whiskers ~ these cats' whiskers ~ we hate these cats*. Of course, where the plural does not end in -*s*, you can tell the genitive singular from the genitive plural from the non-genitive plural even in speech: *the mouse's ears ~ the mice's ears ~ we like these mice*.

Like so many other aspects of morphology, the plurals of nouns are also becoming simpler. If you were asked, 'How do you form a plural noun in English?' you would almost certainly answer, 'Add an -s.' Conventionally, like the genitive, this plural inflectional morpheme is represented as {-S} and nouns which form their plural in this way are said to belong to the **general class**. You will notice that there are different ways of pronouncing the ending. These are allomorphs (see p. 25): /s/ if the singular ends in a voiceless sound, /z/ if the singular ends in a voiced sound and /ɪz/ if the singular ends in a /s/, /z/, /ʃ/, /ʒ/, /tʃ/ or /dʒ/. Which allomorph do you find in these?

matches   parts   boxes   clubs   bees
wishes   cracks   songs
gloves   parties   paths

These general class plurals are not all completely straightforward though. Watch out for some {-S} morphemes which attach in unusual places: *procurators fiscal* (because

procurator is a noun and *fiscal* is an adjective), *courts martial,
mothers-in-law.*

Other ways of forming the plural include changing the
vowel (*mouse ~ mice*). **Invariant plurals** (*sheep ~ sheep*)
remain unchanged. The {-en} class, or **weak class**, has almost
died out, *oxen* being the only true survivor. Another class
which has almost disappeared had the plural inflection {-ru}.
This included English words we can still recognise today:
lambru, calfru, crumbru, which have now joined the general
class, and *cildru*. The {-ru} class was so small that it was no
longer readily recognised as a plural marker and, therefore, to
the last word on the list, our forebears added the {-en}
inflection, when it was still in common use; so today the word
children has two plural endings. The almost obsolete plural
brethren combines an {-en} inflection with a change of vowel.
These last two examples could be described as belonging to a
mixed class.

Many of our loan words originally kept their foreign
plurals. This was particularly true of Latin loans. These are
the commonest Latin types:

sg	pl	sg	pl	sg	pl
-us	*-i*	*-a*	*-ae*	*-um*	*-a*
locus	*loci*	*larva*	*larvae*	*memorandum*	*memoranda*
bacillus	*bacilli*	*papilla*	*papillae*	*bacterium*	*bacteria*
fungus	*fungi*	*lacuna*	*lacunae*	*medium*	*media*

The plural of *stadium* was *stadia*; the plural of *formula* is still,
for some speakers, *formulae* and, although the plural of
fungus is regularly *fungi*, the plural of *crocus* is now *crocuses*.
As the number of people who are familiar with Latin decreases, these plurals are being absorbed into the general class
of nouns. In some loan words, the meanings of the singular
and plural have even begun to diverge. Compare the singular
datum, usually used to refer to a reference point on a map or a
graph, with its plural *data* meaning information. How has the
plural *media* begun to diverge from its singular *medium*? Is
there a difference in meaning between *media* and *mediums*? A

Greek loan word which confuses many people is *phenomenon* in the singular and *phenomena* in the plural. There are a few Italian plurals around too: *graffito* (sg), *graffiti* (pl); *virtuoso* (sg), *virtuosi* (pl).

Invariant nouns should not be confused with **mass nouns** or **non-count** nouns which do not have plurals. These are words like *soup*, *honesty*, *information*. *Deer* is a **count noun**: you can say *one deer* or *ten deer*. You cannot say *two information(s)*. Just to complete the picture, there are a few words which never occur in the singular, like *scissors* and *trousers*.

Note that the absence of an ending is significant in that it marks a noun as singular (except for invariant nouns) and non-genitive.

Adjectives

Adjectives used to be inflected to agree with their noun but now the only inflections that adjectives have are the comparative {-er} and the superlative {-est}: *green, greener, greenest*. There are, however, words usually of more than one syllable to which these endings cannot be added and *more* and *most* must be used: *probable, more probable, most probable*. There are even some adjectives which show **suppletion**. That is when a word of completely different origin is used: *good, better, best; bad, worse, worst*.

Determiners

Again, as you can see from page 67 the inflectional morphology of these too has simplified greatly since Old English times. The OE word for *the* used to change depending on the number and gender of the following noun and even with case. Now the only remnants are the marking of singular and plural in *this ~ these* and *that ~ those*.

CONJUGATION CLASS WORDS

The conjugation class words are the verbs and they can be divided into **finite** and **non-finite** verbs.

Finite verbs

Every well-formed sentence should have one. Finite verbs are marked for **person, number, tense** and **mood**. Consider the difference between *I walk* and *he walks*. That final {-S} works overtime. One of the things it denotes is person. A {-S} marks the third person.

First person	*I walk*
Second person	*you walk*
Third person	*he, she, it walk*s

Note that the lack of {-S} marks *walk* as not third person. The difference between the third person *he walks* and the third person *they walk* is one of number. The {-S} marks the singular. It also marks present tense, *he walks,* by contrasting with the inflection of the past tense, *he walked*, usually designated as {-D}. When an inflection carries more than one piece of information, like this hardworking {-S}, it is an example of **cumulation**. You will notice that there is a lot of syncretism in the verbs. The present tense shows syncretism except in the third person singular, and the past tense has syncretism throughout. Here, again, the morphology of English has been getting simplified as time goes by.

Tense is a grammatical notion. It is not the same thing as time. In terms of inflectional morphology, there are only two tenses in English, the present and the past. If you are wondering what happened to the future, we actually use the present tense to express future time: *I am going to London tomorrow. I go to Paris next week.* We can also use a modal verb: *I will go. I shall go. I should go soon. I may go to Rome next month. I might even stay at home next year.* Modal verbs will be discussed in Chapter 4.

Just as nouns are classified by the way they form plurals, so verbs are classified by the way they form their past tense. The biggest group are the **weak verbs**, which form their past tense by adding {-D}. Allomorphs of this past tense suffix are /d/ after a verb which ends in a voiced sound (*jogged*), /t/ after a verb which ends in a voiceless sound (*walked*) and /ɪd/ after a verb which ends in a /t/ or /d/ (*patted, padded*). The **strong verbs** change their vowel: *come~came, swim~swam*. **Invariant verbs** show no difference between their present tense and past tense: *cut, put*. **Suppletive verbs** are made up of etymologically different words: *go~went*. **Mixed verbs** use more than one of these markers at the same time: *sleep~slept, bring~brought*.

Mood

The **indicative** mood is the one we use most of the time. It contrasts with the **imperative** mood which is used for giving orders or instructions and the **subjunctive** mood which used to be used to express uncertainty or hope. Americans and some conservative British English speakers still use the subjunctive:

> *I suggested that he <u>come</u>.*
> *If a <u>be</u> equal to b then c is equal to d.*
> *I'd be more careful, if I <u>were</u> you.*

For most people, the subjunctive is obsolete and only appears in a few fossilised phrases like *God <u>save</u> the Queen*, and *Heaven <u>help</u> us*.

Non-finite verbs

The name, non-finite, tells you that these verbs are somehow less limited that than finite verbs. They are not constrained by person, number, mood or tense.

The most obvious example is the infinitive. This is the dictionary form of the verb, often preceded by *to*. It takes a zero inflection in PDE: *go, do, think*.

The **past participle** (or, more accurately, the perfect participle, p. 54) of weak verbs looks and sounds the same as the past tense. In other words there is syncretism between the past tense and the past participle:

> *I walked   I have walked*

Strong verbs change their vowel and may also add {-en}:

> *I swam   I have swum*
> *I gave   I have given*
> *I drive   I have driven*

The suppletive verbs, *be* and *go*, have these {-en} past participle inflections: {be} + {-en} = *been*; {go} + {-en} = *gone*.
Present participles end in {-ing}:

> *I am running*.

Finally, the {-ing} suffix can be added to a verb to make a **verbal noun**:

> *Learning morphology is a challenge.*

Here, *learning* is doing a noun's job by being the subject of the sentence. At the same time, it is doing a verb's job by having an object, *morphology*. This is why I have used the term verbal noun instead of the more traditional, but less informative, term, gerund.
Note how the present participle and the past participle can be used as adjectives:

> *A rolling stone gathers no moss.*
> *A watched kettle never boils.*

A complete morphological analysis

We are now in the position to analyse any word in terms of both its derivational and inflectional morphemes:

distrusts

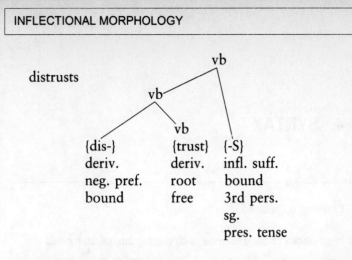

The inflectional suffix shows cumulation. The /s/ allomorph follows a voiceless phoneme.

FURTHER READING

Bauer, L. (1983) *English Word Formation,* Cambridge: Cambridge University Press.
Carstairs-McCarthy, A. (2002) *An Introduction to English Morphology*, Edinburgh: Edinburgh University Press. Highly recommended.
Quirk, R. *et al.* (1985) *A Comprehensive Grammar of the English Language*, London: Longman.

> **Declension class words**: number, case, and, for pronouns, person general class, invariant, vowel change, mixed mass nouns, count nouns
>
> **Conjugation class words**: number, person, tense, mood Finite, non-finite (infinitive, present participle, past participle, verbal noun) Weak, strong, invariant, suppletive, mixed
>
> **Buzz words**: inflection, syncretism, cumulation

4 SYNTAX

Learning outcomes

- to be aware of the existence of different grammatical models

- to identify word classes and understand their function

- to identify the constituents of a sentence and understand the relationships between them

Syntax is that part of the grammar which puts words together. There are a number of different approaches to the subject. Traditional grammarians have tried to lay down prescriptive rules, telling us how we ought to write and speak. Modern grammarians are seeking to find ways of describing what people actually say and why people construct sentences the way they do. Modern grammarians would also like to be able to predict, or generate, any possible sentence. But in trying to draw up rules for generating sentences the question arises as to whether all sentences generated according to these rules could be considered as well formed, possible sentences that anyone would really say or write and expect to be understood. There are sentences which obey all the so-called 'rules' but are so involved or lengthy that they become incomprehensible:

The lecturer the professor taught taught my sister.

or

*This is the man all tattered and torn that married the
maiden all forlorn that milked the cow with the crumpled
horn that chased the dog that worried the cat that killed
the rat that ate the malt that lay in the house that Jack
built.*

Can such sentences be said to be grammatical? There is
obviously a gap between what we know to be correctly generated according to rules and our ability to process these rules in
all circumstances. This gap raises all sorts of interesting questions. Noam Chomsky, one of the major figures in the development of modern ways of looking at syntax used the terms
competence and **performance** and you will find these terms used
by many syntacticians including Huddleston (1976).

What is studied under the heading of 'English Grammar' at
university has therefore not got a lot to do with 'grammatical
correctness' as lay people understand it. The starting point is
not some sort of prescriptive rule book which says 'this is how
you must speak and write'. Instead, the starting point is the
competence of native speakers which enables them to interpret
sentences and judge them intuitively as well formed or not well
formed. Anyone who speaks English can recognise that

There is nothing wrong with this sentence.

is well formed but is in no doubt that there is something
unacceptable about

*There nothing wrong is this sentence with.

(It is conventional to mark ungrammatical sentences with an
asterisk.) Consider, however the sentence:

There ain't nothing wrong with this sentence.

Is it well formed? It depends what dialect the speaker is using.
It is not a well-formed sentence for speakers of Standard
English, but that does not make it wrong for the dialect

speaker. Well-formedness, like all other aspects of English Language, changes with region, with time, and even with situation. What the modern grammarian is trying to do is find ways of describing grammar that tie in with native speakers' intuitions. In so doing, they should be able to shed light on the way we think about and acquire language and give us an insight into the workings of the human mind. That is a pretty tall order. It is not surprising that, as yet, there is no single solution.

There is much debate among scholars as to the best way to tackle grammar and there is no one grammar which works perfectly all the time. As with most academic areas of dispute, there is a lot to be learned from all approaches and, as your knowledge increases, you will become able to read more critically and perhaps even contribute to the debate. What follows in this chapter is largely based on a phrase-structure grammar which is a very useful start to describing how sentences are put together. Huddleston (1976), Hudson (1998) and Miller (2002) take very different approaches and you may like to compare them with Burton-Roberts (1997).

PARSING (WORD CLASSES)

Words can be grouped into categories or classes, often called word classes. There are some definitions for the parts of speech which have been around for a long time. Although they are rather oversimplified, they are quite a good place to start if you have never done any grammar before. Even if you have learnt the word classes already, you might find it useful just to check that you know all this. You may find a few surprises.

Noun

A noun is a naming word. **Animate nouns** are used to name a person or animal. **Inanimate nouns** are used for the naming of things. **Abstract nouns** are things you cannot see or touch, like *idea,* and the opposite of an abstract noun is a **concrete noun,** like *book.* Proper nouns are personal names, place names, organisation names and so on, with a capital letter. If a noun is not a proper noun, then it is a **common noun.** Nouns can also be subdivided in to **count** nouns and **non-count** or **mass** nouns. Count nouns, as the name suggests, are discrete and individual things that can be counted, like *apples* and *cars.* Mass nouns, by contrast, are things that come in quantities rather than as individuals, like *soup, snow* and *information.* As noted in the chapter on morphology (p. 33), mass nouns do not form plurals.

Verb

A verb is often described as a doing word. This definition has severe limitations. Many students who use this definition have great difficulty spotting some verbs like *be,* because, as one student put it, *be* is a 'being word', not a 'doing word'. Not surprisingly, she also had problems with *may, can, should* and so on. Sometimes you need to look closely at what a word is doing in a sentence before you can decide. You can get some clues from the chapter on inflectional morphology (Chapter 3). For example, only verbs have tense. The fact that the difference between *he is* and *he was* is one of present tense versus past tense tells you that *is* and *was* are verbs. When we go on to look at the structure of verb phrases, you will find other clues to help you recognise a verb.

Pronoun

It is usually said that a **pronoun** stands in place of a noun, but compare the sentences

She ate <u>a huge pink and white ice-cream with a cherry on the top</u>.

and

  She ate it.

The pronoun *it* replaces a lot more than just the noun itself. It replaces the entire phrase that belongs to the noun and so we must rephrase our definition of a pronoun and say that a pronoun stands in place of a noun phrase.

  I, you, him and so on are **personal pronouns**. *Who, which, that, whose* can also replace a noun phrase and they are known as **relative pronouns**:

  This is the house. Jack built the house.
  This is the house that Jack built.

Then there are the interrogative pronouns:

  What did you say? Who was that?

Finally, there are the **reflexive pronouns**:

  I wash myself. They dress themselves.

Adjective

An **adjective** can be said to describe, or **modify**, a noun (*red, proud, happy*).

  The red book.

Again, there is a bit of oversimplification going on here. If we consider the phrase *a pink, scaly monster*, there is no doubt that *scaly* modifies *monster*, but what about *pink*? It actually modifies *scaly monster*, not just *monster* itself. Let's consider all monsters. Some monsters are scaly. So let us limit our consideration to scaly monsters. Of all the scaly monsters in the world, some are pink, and we want to consider the pink subset of all scaly monsters. So an adjective can modify a noun, or it can modify something rather more than a noun, namely a noun plus its other modifier(s).

Adjectives can also modify a complete noun phrase, or the pronoun which stands in for a noun phrase.

> *The panoramic view from the top of the mountain is* <u>*beautiful*</u>.
> *I am* <u>*happy*</u>.

Adverb

Traditionally, an **adverb** (*happily, slowly, fast*), is said to modify a verb but consider this sentence:

> <u>*Sadly*</u>, *she cooks spaghetti* <u>*badly*</u>.

This sentence is not saying that she cooks badly; she may cook tagliatelli rather well. The adverb *badly* is modifying the entire phrase *cooks spaghetti*. She may cook happily. The adverb *sadly* is modifying the entire sentence. Yet again, the traditional definition simply will not do. Also under the heading of adverb is the **degree adverb**, a class of words which modify other adverbs or adjectives. These are words like *very* and *extremely* and *slightly*.

> *It was* <u>*bitterly*</u> *cold and so we dressed* <u>*quite*</u> *warmly*.

Preposition

Prepositions can show relationships in space and time. You may feel this definition is not particularly helpful, and you would be right! It may help if you keep your propositions *<u>in</u> a box*. Then you can put them <u>*under*</u> *the box*, <u>*above*</u> *the box*, <u>*beside*</u> *the box*, <u>*into*</u> *the box*, <u>*through*</u> *the box*, <u>*before*</u> *the box*, <u>*after*</u> *the box* etc. Most of these examples express spatial

relationship. The last two usually refer to temporal relationships. Different relationships are expressed in *of the box*, *for
the box*, *with the box*, *like the box*. Prepositions may consist of
more than one word: *out of* the box. The best way to identify a
preposition is to look at the kind of phrase it is part of. It is the
head of a prepositional phrase and a prepositional phrase
always consists of a preposition followed by a noun phrase.
Before you read any further, read the last two sentences again
and meditate. Why is *up* not a preposition in *I wish you'd do
the washing up!*? Why is it a proposition in *He hid the book up
his jumper*?

Conjunction

Words, phrases and sentences may be joined by **conjunctions**.
If the two things on either side of the conjunction are of equal
status, the conjunction is a **co-ordinating** conjunction. *And*,
but and *or* are co-ordinating conjunctions. If you join two
sentences with a **subordinating** conjunction, like *because*,
when, *whenever*, *where*, *if*, you make one of the sentences
less important, adding a comment on the other:

  I ate a cake.
  I was hungry.
  I ate a cake because I was hungry.

I ate a cake is the main **clause** and *because I was hungry*
becomes a subordinate clause. (A clause may be defined as a
structural unit smaller than a sentence but bigger than a
phrase.)

Articles and so on

Then, what are we to do with *a, the, that, those, these, this,
one, two, three, some*? Well, we could call *a* the **indefinite
article**, *the* the **definite article**, *that, those, this* and *these*

demonstratives, *one*, *two*, *three* numerals and *some* a quantifier, but all these words, as we shall see, perform the same
function within a sentence. Their word classes involve a lot of
terminology but at least we can gather them together under the
single function name, **determiner**. The possessive form of the
personal pronoun (*my*, *your*, *his* and so on) also functions as a
determiner. A singular noun referring to something that can be
counted must have a determiner. The sentence

The cat slept on a cushion.

would be ungrammatical without the *the* or the *a*. What other
words could you use in their place? With plural nouns and
non-count, or mass, nouns like *soup* or *information*, the
determiner is optional. This leads us on to questions of word
order, phrase structure and function.

Parsing exercise

See if you can parse the words in the following sentence.

Peter picked a peck of pickled pepper very properly.

Once you have read the rest of the chapter, try again and this
time give reasons for your decisions. You'll find the answers at
the end of this chapter.

WORD ORDER

A sentence is not just a random list of words. The different
parts of speech are combined in an accepted order. The
determiner comes before the noun. The adjective comes after
the determiner and before the noun as in *the black dog*. There
is a strict word order in English sentences which tells us what
the functions are of various parts of the sentence. How can
you combine the following words?

the the elephants mice chase

The two possibilities are

The mice chase the elephants

and

The elephants chase the mice.

It is only the word order which tells us who is doing the chasing and who is being chased.

CONSTITUENTS

The words are put together in units called constituents. Small constituents are arranged in bigger constituents. The bigger constituents are assembled into even bigger constituents until the sentence is complete. You can recognise constituents because they follow regular patterns. That is to say, each constituent is formed according to a set of rules.

What are the constituents of this sentence?

The boy with black hair watched the tall girl with unblinking eyes.

You will instantly see bits that you would instinctively want to keep together. If we analyse this sentence in a methodical way, you will see if your instincts were right.The two big constituents of a well-formed sentence are known as the **subject** and the **predicate**. Usually the subject is what the sentence is about and the predicate says (or predicates) something about the subject. So, in this case, the subject is *the boy with black hair* and the predicate is *watched the tall girl with unblinking eyes*. (Unfortunately, in a sentence like *It is a nice day* the word *it* can hardly be said to be what the sentence is about but it is still the grammatical subject because it is *it* which determines that the form of the verb will be *is* rather than *are* or *am*.)

Subject and predicate exercise

Divide the following sentences into subject and predicate. (Answers at the end of the chapter.)

Marjorie swims.
Fantastic Fred fed the ducks.
The ducks on the pond and all their little ducklings chased Fred and Marjorie.
She blamed him for their misfortune.

Smaller constituents

What are the constituents of the predicate? How would you divide up *watched the tall girl with unblinking eyes*? If you can't see where to divide things up, try asking a different question: what really wants to stick together? *With unblinking eyes* certainly looks as if it is has been preassembled as a constituent. That leaves us with two possible orders in which to glue the bits together:

watched the tall girl + with unblinking eyes

or

watched + the tall girl with unblinking eyes.

The first solution makes the satisfyingly complete phrase *watched the tall girl,* and *The boy with black hair watched the tall girl* makes a perfectly good sentence on its own. Given this reading of the sentence, *with unblinking eyes* appears as a sort of optional extra describing the whole phrase *watched the tall girl.* The second solution has *with the unblinking eyes* attached to *girl*. Both analyses make sense but the constituents are different. Continuing with the first solution, *watched the tall girl* splits into the two smaller constituents, *watched* and *the tall girl*. Now do we want *the tall* or *tall girl*? I'm sure you will agree that the adjective combines with the noun to give *tall girl* and the determiner is added last. An incomplete noun phrase without its determiner is a **nominal**.

If we analyse the predicate according to our second solution, we have to start dividing up *the tall girl with unblinking eyes*. We know that this is a noun phrase. We have just seen how a noun phrase consists of a determiner and a nominal. If we try that, we get the two constituents, a determiner *the* and a nominal *tall girl with unblinking eyes*. Our next big decision is whether we want *tall girl + with unblinking eyes* or *tall + girl with unblinking eyes*. If you cast your mind back to an earlier example, *a pink, scaly monster*, it was suggested that *pink* modified *scaly monster* because pink, scaly monsters formed a subset of scaly monsters, which, of course are a subset of all monsters. In the case of *the tall girl with unblinking eyes*, girls with unblinking eyes are a subset of all girls and out of that subset, we are going to select a tall one. So our constituents are *tall + girl with unblinking eyes*. Whichever solution we choose, finding the constituents of *with unblinking eyes* poses no problems. Obviously *unblinking eyes* is a constituent and *with* is a constituent. Here we have a preposition followed by a noun phrase, just as it should be.

If we analyse the subject, the determiner *the* separates off from the nominal, *boy with black hair*. *With black hair* is describing *boy*. *With* is a proposition and *black hair* is a noun phrase.

This sounds very complicated but it is easy enough if you just take a step at a time.

Think about how you could divide the following phrases into their constituents. The first one is done for you. The answers to the rest are at the end of the chapter.

a very happy birthday
(a) (very happy birthday) determiner + nominal

(*very happy*) (*birthday*) *very* modifies *happy* and together they make an adjective phrase which modifies *birthday*.

The top split in this tree separates *a* from *very happy birthday*. The next split down separates *very happy* from *birthday*. Lastly, *very* and *happy* are split. You could look at it the other way: *very* goes with *happy*. We have made a bigger constituent *very happy* which we then join with *birthday* to give *very happy birthday* and finally, we tag on the *a*. It doesn't matter whether you see the following exercise as an exercise in taking things apart or putting them back together, just so long as you can spot constituents.

> *a forged ten pound note*
> *extra-marital sex*
> *extra big bum bags*
> *fifty odd inhabitants*
> *old men and women*
> *the agitated cat on the hot tin roof*

FUNCTIONS OF CONSTITUENT PHRASES

The noun phrase

The noun phrase consists of a head noun, any adjectives or prepositional phrases which describe, or **modify**, the head noun, and a determiner. A noun phrase can act as the subject of a sentence. It can also appear as a necessary part of the predicate as an object, an object predicative or a subject predicative (see verb phrase, below). It can even modify a verb phrase: *I arrived last week*. Another function of the noun phrase, which we have already seen, is to combine with a preposition in a prepositional phrase. Do not be surprised if a noun phrase consists of only one word: *John arrived*. Even the pronoun which replaces an ordinary noun phrase is labelled as a noun phrase. Here are some examples of noun phrase structures:

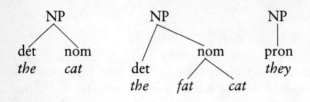

The verb phrase

The head word of a verb phrase is the verb and the structure of the rest of the verb phrase depends on the kind of verb it follows. Some verbs can stand alone. Others can or must take some kind of **complement**. What follows is a rather too brief discussion of verb complementation. It might make sense to you instantly, if you have that kind of mind, but do not worry if this is hard going; some kinds of verbs are easier to spot than others and you will get lots of supervised practice in this type of thing. Also, you may find that some books use different terms but the concepts are far more important than the jargon.

1. Consider:
   I slept.
   You sunbathed.

Both of these sentences are perfectly well formed and the verb phrase can consist of the verb just on its own. Such verbs are called **intransitive**. That simply means that they do not take an object. (You could describe this in a very shorthand way by saying VP = V)

2. Now consider
   *I made.
   *You expected.

These sentences are not well formed. What this verb needs is an **object** to complete it.

> *I made a cake.*
> *You expected rain.*

These are **monotransitive** verbs. They take a single object (VP = VO).

3. There are **ditransitive** verbs which can take two objects:
   He sent me a letter.
   He made me a cup of tea.

With ditransitive verbs, one of the objects is traditionally called the **direct object** and the other, the one to or for which the action is performed, is called the **indirect object**. So, in the two sentences above, *a letter* and *a cup of tea* are the direct objects and *me* is the indirect object (VP = VOO).

4. Notice how the sentence
   He made me a cup of tea.

is different from

> *He made me a legend in my own lifetime.*

In this last sentence, the noun phrase *a legend in my own lifetime* refers to *me*. *Me* is an object but *a legend in my own lifetime* says something about the object and so it is called an **object predicative** (oP). We can add object predicative to our list of things that a noun phrase can do. Adjective phrases and prepositional phrases can also act as object predicatives:

> *He made her very happy.* (object = *her*; object predicative = *very happy*)
> *She turned him into a syntactician.* (object = *him*; object predicative = *into a syntactician*)

Verbs which take an object and an object predicative are
complex transitive (VP = VOoP).

5. There is yet another group of verbs known as **intensive
   verbs**. They are followed not by an object but by a
   subject predicative (sP). The subject predicative can be a
   noun phrase, an adjective phrase or a prepositional
   phrase referring to the subject:
   I am an idiot.
   Poirot grew suspicious.
   The violin sounded in tune.
   (VP = VsP)

6. Finally, there are the **prepositional verbs**. There is
   definitely something incomplete about
   *He glanced

If you think of all the things you could add to make this a well-
formed sentence, they are prepositional phrases: *over his
specs; out of the window; up the chimney.* (VP = VprepP)
Compare very carefully:

   He looked up the chimney.
   He looked up her address.

In the first of these sentences, *up the chimney* is a constituent.
In the second sentence *looked up* is a constituent. So the first
sentence is a prepositional sentence and the second is monotransitive. Which would you apply to this sentence?

   He looked up an old friend.

Complementation exercise

As you will have noticed, there are some verbs which are
stuck firmly in one group – they can only take one kind of

complementation. With others, more than one type of complementation is possible and you have to decide on the basis of the sentence in front of you. (Remember this when you come to read about adverbials.) Look at the verb complementation in the following sentences and name the kind of verb:

1. *Mary called me a taxi.*
2. *John called me a star.*
3. *Bears like honey.*
4. *I slept in.*
5. *I feel out of sorts.*
6. *He applied for a driving licence.*
7. *The water becomes hot.*
8. *The ice-cream froze.*
9. *He has put his cards on the table.*
10. *He has swallowed a whole onion.*
11. *Give him mouth-to-mouth resuscitation.*
12. *We'll make him better.*
13. *Too late, he has expired.*
14. *That is a great pity.*
15. *We told the sexton.*
16. *The sexton tolled the bell.*

AUXILIARY VERBS

English uses auxiliary verbs to do some of the things that other languages do with inflections.

Aspect

The simple aspect is the unmarked form where there is neither *be* nor *have* used in the way described below. *Be* and *have* are primary auxiliaries. They are used to express **aspect,** that is to say the **progressive** aspect using *be* followed by the **present participle** as in

He is singing.
She was running.

and the **perfect** aspect which is expressed with *have* followed
by the **perfect participle** (sometimes called the past participle)
as in

He has sung.
She had run.

The primary auxiliary *be* followed by the **passive participle**
(sometimes just called the past participle and identical in form
to the perfect participle) is used to turn an **active** sentence into
a passive sentence. Active and passive are referred to as **voice**.
Note that the noun phrase which is the object in the active
sentence becomes the grammatical subject in the passive
sentence and the original subject becomes an optional adverbial prepositional phrase:

Active: *The dog chases the cat.*
Passive: *The cat is chased (by the dog).*

It follows that only transitive verbs (monotransitive, ditransitive or complex transitive) can be used to form
passives, since there must be an object there in the active
sentence.

The other primary auxiliary is *do* which we need to form
questions and negatives. In Shakespeare's time you could have
said *Sing you?* or *You sing not.* In PDE, you need to use the
auxiliary *do* (*Do you sing? You do not sing.*) unless there is
another auxiliary there already (*You are singing. Are you
singing? You have not sung. Can you sing?*)

The **modal auxiliaries** express **mood** or **modality**. They are
can, could, may, might, must, shall, used to, will and so on.
Modals are very strange verbs. For one thing, some of them
carry a number of different meanings. What does *could* mean
in the following examples?

I could play tennis before I broke my leg.
Could you close the window, please?
Could I have a drink of water?
We could go out tonight, if you're not doing anything.
We'd better not have a party. The landlady could come
back early.

Shall and *will* can be used to express futurity. As we have seen, time is not the same thing as tense. In this sense, *shall* is used with the first person only but *will* can be used with any person. Because they are both usually reduced to *'ll*, you cannot tell them apart in spoken language, although many people, particularly in the south of England use *I shall* and *we shall* in formal writing and *Shall I?* is the interrogative form which is used in the south. What else can *will* do? Consider the following.

That'll be right!
Will you come into my parlour?
Will you shut up!

Can you describe the exact meaning of *will* in each example?

Another peculiar thing about modal verbs is the way that past and present tense does not quite work. For one thing, some modals like *must* do not have a past and *used to* doesn't have a present tense. For another thing, the past and present meanings are not always equivalent in meaning. Sometimes *should* is regarded as the past tense of *shall*, but is it really? *I shall do my homework* makes me feel reasonably confident that the homework will be done. *I should do my homework* is in no way a past tense, and there is no guarantee this time that there is any intention to get started. Clearly, there is no past/present relationship between these two sentences.

Auxiliaries can be combined but, if they are, there are rules which are always obeyed. The first in the sequence is the finite verb. It carries tense and agrees with the subject in person and number. Note how each one in the sequence dictates the non-finite form of the verb which follows.

- The modal takes the infinitive (*I can walk.*)

- The perfect takes the past participle (*I have walked. He has gone.*)

- The progressive takes the present participle (*I am walking.*)

- The passive takes the past participle (*The door was opened.*)

(Some people distinguish between the perfect or perfective participle and the passive participle, but the forms are the same.)

Where auxiliary verbs appear, they always follow the same order:

- modal

- perfect

- progressive

- passive.

> *I fed the cat.* (past tense, no modal, simple aspect, active voice)
> *I will be feeding the cat.* (present tense, modal, progressive aspect, active voice)
> *The cat could have been being fed.* (past tense, modal, perfect, progressive, passive)

If you have learned a foreign language at school, you may have been taught that *I have gone* is perfect and *I had gone* is pluperfect and *I will have gone* is future perfect. This terminology works very well for Latin which does all these things with inflections but, for a language like English which uses auxiliary verbs, such terms are really not very helpful.

Adverbials

Modifiers of the verb phrase are known as adverbials. Adverbs, prepositional phrases and noun phrases can all act as adverbials. As modifiers, they are optional, unlike complements which are necessary parts of a constituent.

He slept (deeply) (in a bunk bed) (in the blue bedroom) (last night). Four optional extras. *She glanced at the book (before she spoke)*. Only the last prepositional phrase is an optional modifier. The first is the necessary complement to complete the verb phrase.

It is important to distinguish between complements – which are grammatically part of the completion of the verb phrase – and modifiers, which are additional extras.

Adverbial vs complement

Classify the underlined phrases in the following sentences as complements or modifiers and identify the kind of verb:

> *He turned <u>nasty</u>.*
> *He turned <u>sharply</u>.*
> *He turned <u>at the doorway</u>.*
> *He turned <u>the steering wheel</u>.*
> *He turned the water <u>into wine</u>.*

ANSWERS TO EXERCISES

Parsing exercise

a) *Peter* is a proper noun. (Name of a person. It is also the subject of the sentence. Subjects have to be noun phrases. So *Peter*, as the headword of a noun phrase, must be a noun.)

b) *Picked* is a verb. (It is a 'doing' word. It also has tense which is something that only verbs have. It is also the headword of the verb phrase.)

c) *a* is the indefinite article. (For no better reason than that is something you learn. It is functioning as a determiner because is necessary to make a complete noun phrase when joined with a nominal.)

d) *peck* is a noun. (Name of a thing. It is also the headword of the phrase *a peck of pickled pepper*. This phrase is the object and an object must be a noun phrase and its headword must be a noun. Note that *peck* in a different sentence such as *The birds peck the corn* could be a verb.)

e) *of* is a preposition. (Try the 'box' test – *of the box*. It forms a complete phrase with the following noun phrase which supports the idea that this is indeed a preposition.)

f) *pickled* is actually a past (or more precisely a passive) participle. (The morphology shows it is formed from the verb *to pickle*. In this sentence it is behaving like an adjective, modifying *pepper*.)

g) *pepper* is a noun. (It is the name of a thing. It is also the head of the noun phrase that must follow the preposition to make a prepositional phrase. In another sentence it might act as a verb: *They salt and pepper their tomatoes*. Could you say why *salt* and *pepper* must be verbs here?)

h) *very* is a degree adverb. (It is modifying the following adverb.)

i) *properly* is an adverb. (It is the headword of the adverbial phrase *very properly* which modifies the verb phrase *picked a peck of picked pepper*.)

Subject and predicate exercise

Marjorie | *swims.*
Fantastic Fred | *fed the ducks.*
The ducks on the pond and all their little ducklings | *chased Fred and Marjorie.*
She | *blamed him for all their misfortune.*

You will notice that the length of the subject and the length of the predicate are very variable.

Constituency exercise

(a) (*forged ten pound note*) article + nominal
(*forged*) (*ten pound note*) *forged* modifies all of *ten pound note*
(*ten pound*) (*note*) not a *pound note* x 10 but a *note* for *ten pound*(s)

(*extra*) (*marital sex*) for more of a good thing but (*extra marital*) (*sex*) leads to nothing but trouble!

(*extra large*)(*bum bag*) was probably your first thought, but you could make it bumbags for extra-large bums or additional bumbags in a large size.

(*fifty odd*) (*inhabitants*) implies a population numbering between 45 and 55 without any marked peculiarities.

(*old*) (*men and women*) if they are all old.
(*old men*) (*and*)(*women*) if the women are of unspecified age.

(*the*) (*agitated cat on the hot tin roof*) article + nominal
(*agitated*) (*cat on the hot tin roof*) In constructions of this type, it usually makes more sense to ask 'Which *cat on the hot tin roof*'? rather than 'Which *agitated cat*?'
(*cat*) (*on the hot tin roof*) noun + prepositional phrase
(*on*) (*the hot tin roof*) preposition + noun phrase
(*the*) (*hot tin roof*) determiner + nominal
(*hot*) (*tin roof*) *hot* modifies all of *tin roof*

Complementation exercise

1. Ditransitive (VOO) 2. Complex transitive (VOoP) 3. Mono-transitive (VO) 4. Intransitive (V) 5. Intensive (VsP) 6. Pre-positional (VprepP) 7. Intensive (VsP) 8. Intransitive (V) 9. Complex transitive (VOoP) 10. Monotransitive (VO) 11 Ditransitive (VOO) 12. Complex transitive (VOoP) 13. In-transitive (V) 14. Intensive (VsP) 15. Monotransitive (VO) 16. Monotransitive (VO)

Adverbial vs complement

Intensive + adjective phrase subject predicative as complement
Intransitive + adverbial phrase modifier
Intransitive + prepositional phrase modifier
Monotransitive + noun phrase object as complement
Complex transitive with a noun phrase as the object and a prepositional phrase as an object predicative. These are both complements.

FURTHER READING

Burton-Roberts, N. (1997) *Analysing Sentences*, London: Longman. This contains plenty of exercises and, not only does he give you answers, but he also points out where you are likely to have gone wrong and why.

Huddleston, R. (1984) *Introduction to the Grammar of English*, Cambridge: Cambridge University Press. Another very approachable book which looks at transformational syntax.

Hudson, R. (1998) *English Grammar*, London: Routledge. This is well worth looking at. It is by far the most accessible introduction to dependency grammar.

Miller, J. (2002) *An Introduction to English Syntax*, Edinburgh: Edinburgh University Press. Probably the easiest to start with. Very readable.

Quirk, R. et al. (1985) *A Comprehensive Grammar of the English Language*, London: Longman. This is a traditional reference book, useful for looking things up or simply browsing.

Parts of speech: nouns, verbs, pronouns, adjectives, adverbs, propositions, conjunctions, articles

Constituents
Subject and predicate
Noun phrases
Verb phrases

Complementation: intransitive, monotransitive, ditransitive, complex transitive, intensive
  Prepositional (V, VO, VOO, VOoP, VsP, VprepP)

Aspect: simple, progressive, perfect

Voice: active, passive

5 THE HISTORY OF ENGLISH

Learning outcomes

● to know the main chronological periods of English and relate them to external historical events

● to recognise and describe some of the features of each period using the skills acquired in the preceding chapters

English is one of the Germanic family of languages. It is therefore closely related to High and Low German, Dutch and the Scandinavian languages. After the Romans retreated from Britain in 410 AD, Angles, Saxons and Jutes began to settle in England in large numbers, gradually overcoming the British Celtic-speaking tribes, pushing them and their language into Wales and Cornwall by the end of the sixth century. And this is when the history of English begins.

OLD ENGLISH (to about 1100)

External history

The Jutes settled mainly in Kent. The Saxons took possession of the rest of southern England and the Anglians pushed north to form the kingdoms of Mercia and Northumbria and gradually advanced into Scotland. Even at the earliest date, there is evidence for dialectal differences among the speakers of Old English (OE), or Anglo-Saxon as it is also called. With the spread of Christianity, through the efforts of the Irish monk Columba and his followers in the north, and under the influence of Augustine in the South, written texts in a Latin-based alphabet began to appear. From the eighth century, the Vikings started to make raids on eastern England and, in the ninth century, had it not been for the persistence of Alfred the Great, they might have overrun England completely. He held out in the south and west and by the Treaty of Wedmore (878 AD) a Viking kingdom was established as the Danelaw in the north-east of England and they were, more or less, kept there until the very end of the tenth century when Olaf of Norway and Svein of Denmark joined forces. Svein claimed the English throne from Æthelred in 1014. His son Cnut secured the throne in 1016 and the Danes ruled England until Edward the Confessor became king in 1042. Nevertheless, the area which was most influenced by contact with the Danes was the north-east. The end of the Old English Period was heralded by the Norman Conquest.

A Sample of OE

Ælc þara þe þas min word gehierþ and þa wyrcþ biþ gelic þæm wisan were se his hus ofer stan getimbrode. Þa com þær regen and micel flod and þær bleowon windas and ahruron on þæt hus and hit na ne feoll. Soþlice hit wæs ofer stan getimbrod.

(Each of these who those my words hear and them work is like the wise man who his house over stone built. Then came there rain and a great flood and there blew winds and beat on that house and it not not fell. Truly it was over stone built.)

This word-for-word translation will help you to identify some of the similarities as well as some of the differences.

Phonology and spelling

There are a number of ways of reconstructing the pronunciation of OE. One way is to look at related languages and try to work back through changes in pronunciation to an earlier stage, but by far the most straightforward evidence comes from spelling. The Germanic peoples had their own writing system, runes, but these were designed for carving on stone, wood or bone and their straight lines were not very convenient for writing at length on parchment or vellum. When the Irish monks adapted their Latin-based alphabet for writing Old English, it is reasonable to assume that they set about it in a systematic way and tried, as far as possible, to have one symbol to represent each phoneme. This was not easy because each language has its own set of phonemes and Old English had a few sounds that Latin did not have. In the case of /θ/, they solved the problem by using the runic symbol thorn <þ>. (In fact, they came up with two solutions for /θ/ and used the eth <ð> symbol as well.) Just in case you have an ambition to read the passage aloud, here is a key to what they did, but you are unlikely to be expected to know the phonology of OE in so much detail in your first year.

<a> represents short /a/ and long /aː/. The : is an IPA symbol indicating that a vowel is long.
<e> represents short /e/ and long /eː/ and schwa /ə/.
<i> and <ie> represent short /i/ and long /iː/.
<o> represents short /o/ and long /oː/
<u> represents short /u/ and long /uː/
<æ> represents the Old English phoneme /æ/, a vowel between /ɛ/ and /a/ such as Americans and very conservative RP speakers use in *cat*, and its long counterpart /æː/.
<y> represents /y/, a high front-rounded vowel between /i/ and /u/. It too may be long or short.

The consonants are just as easy:

<b, d, f, k, l, m, n, p, r, s, t, w> present no problems.

<c> is /k/ unless it is followed by a front vowel or /ə/ when it becomes /tʃ/ as in PDE *child* /tʃaɪld/ = OE *cild* /tʃiː ld/.

<g> represents two sounds, either /ɣ/, a voiced velar fricative, which you might like to try to say, or /j/ as in PDE *yes*.

<h> is /x/, a voiceless velar fricative.

<þ> and <ð> both represent the voiceless dental fricative /θ/. There was no voiced dental fricative in OE.

You will notice some differences in the phoneme inventory. There are a few extra phonemes and a few others, like the voiced dental and alveolar fricatives, are absent.

Vocabulary

In the sample passage, some words are instantly recognisable, like *word, his, windas*. Others are not so very different from their modern versions: *bleowan, ofer, feoll*. *Hus* and *stan* present no problems for Scottish readers. *Wer* is the word for 'man' that we still use in *werewolf*. The Anglo-Saxons had few loan words. They preferred to create new words by affixation and compounding from their own Germanic word stock. Although, unfortunately, there are no examples in this short passage, they had some delightful compounds such as *leorningcnihtas* (learning knights or learning young men) rather than the Latin loan *disciples* that we use today. Old English poetry is full of vivid metaphors formed by compounding such as *hronrad* (whale-road) for 'sea'. Some OE affixes that you might recognise are {-full}, {-leas}, {-nes}, {mis-}, {be-} and {under-}.

Some Latin loans date from the time when the Angles, Saxons and Jutes were still on mainland Europe, words like *camp* (battle) and *cese* (cheese). Remember, however, that the Romans had gone home before the Anglo-Saxons got here and so there was no direct contact between Romans and OE speakers in Britain. However, OE did borrow a number of Latin words after the Anglo-Saxons were converted to

Christianity. Many of these were to do with the church, such as *abbod*, but some more general words were also borrowed, like *lent* (lentil). But even in religious matters, it is quite remarkable how creative the Anglo-Saxons were in using their own native resources to describe new concepts. They used *halig gast* rather than adapting the Latin *spiritus sanctus* and the Trinity was simply translated into OE as *þrines* (three-ness). Following the conventions of OE poetry, they found lots of religious synonyms. In *The Dream of the Rood*, a very beautiful and subtle poem about the crucifixion, in which a dreamer sees the cross and hears it tell its own story, some of the words that are used for Christ are *wealdend* (ruler), *hælend* (healer or saviour), *frean mancynnes* (mankind's lord), *dryhten* (lord), *geong hæleð* (young hero), *heofona hlaford* (heaven's lord, from *hlaf-weard* literally 'loaf-keeper') and *ricne cyning* (the king of the kingdom). You can get an inkling from some of these words of the way in which they reflect Anglo-Saxon society in which you were dependent on your lord, whom you would defend even at the cost of your own life, and in which a man without a lord was at best treated with suspicion.

Although the Danish invasions and settlement took place during the OE period, there is little evidence of Scandinavian influence in OE texts. The texts we have from the tenth and eleventh centuries are quite formal texts and words of Scandinavian origin were most likely to be borrowed in informal spoken contexts. These loans really come into their own in the Middle English period.

Inflectional morphology

Inflectional morphology was a lot more complicated in OE. Looking first at the declension class words, where we now have natural gender, OE had grammatical gender so, although *word, hus* and *flod* are neuter, *stan* and *wind* are masculine. The difference between *þæm* in *þæm wisan were* and *þæt* in *on þæt hus* is that *þæm* agrees with a noun that is masculine singular dative and *þæt* agrees with neuter singular accusative noun. Even the adjective *wisan* is inflected. If we take *the stone* in OE and look at all the forms it can take, we will get some idea of how important inflectional morphology is in OE.

Case	sg.	pl.
Nominative (subject)	*se stan*	*þa stanas*
Accusative (object)	*þone stan*	*þa stanas*
Genitive (possessive)	*þæs stanes*	*þara stana*
Dative (indirect object)	*þæm stane*	*þæm stanum*

So:

Se wer stood on the hill.	*þa weras* stood on the hill.
I greeted *þone wer*.	I greeted *þa weras*.
þæs weres hair was grey.	*þara wera* hair was grey.
Give it to *þæm were*.	Give it to *þæm werum*.

Strong masculine nouns like *stan* and *wer* formed the largest class of nouns in OE. This class is the ancestor of our general class in PDE. You can see where our modern genitive singular {-S} ending comes from. The nominative and the accusative are much more commonly used than the genitive and dative, with the result that, by analogy, the plural {-a} and {-um} endings were replaced with the more common {-S} and we ended up with the plural we have today.

In the conjugation class words, also, there is much less syncretism than we have today. The third person singular present tense is {-e}. You can see the weak past tense {-D} in *getimbrode,* but the final {-e} says third person singular, even with a weak past tense, something that has been lost in Present Day English (PDE). *Com* and *feoll* are strong verbs.

Syntax

The word order looks more like German than PDE with the main verb at the end in subordinate clauses and the subject and verb reversed after adverbials. Two negatives do not make a positive. If fact, negatives were cumulative and the more negatives you used, the more definitely you meant 'no'.

EARLY MIDDLE ENGLISH (about 1100–about 1300)

External history

The main trigger for the transition between OE and Middle English was the Norman Conquest. Although French speakers were numerically never more than 10 per cent of the population, and may have been fewer, they were in positions of authority in government, in the church and in all spheres of influence. It was Latin, rather than French, that replaced English in government documents and scarcely any written English survives from the period immediately after the Norman Conquest. When it resurfaces, it is much more recognisable and a modern reader, with some help from a glossary, should be able to read it without too much difficulty. Here is a short passage from the *Peterborough Chronicle* describing events in the year 1137 but written some time after 1154:

> Tha namen hi the men the hi wenden ðat ani god hefden, bathe be nihtes and be daies, carlmen and wimmen, and diden heom in prisun and pined heom efter gold and syluer untellendlice pining, for ne uuæren næure nan martyrs swa pined als hi wæron. Me henged up be the fet and smoked heom mid ful smoke. Me henged bi the thumbes other bi the hefed and hengen bryniges on her fet. Me dide cnotted strenges abuton here hæued and uurythen it ðat it gæde to ðe hærnes. Hi diden heom in quarterne ðar nadres and snakes and pades wæron inne, and drapen heom swa.

Vocabulary

Now the Anglo-Saxon words like *namen* (took), *wenden* (thought), *niht* (night), *quarterne* (dungeon), *pined* (tortured), *untellendlice* (unspeakable, beyond telling) and *bryniges* (cuirasses, corselets), are beginning to be joined by Norman French loan words such as *prisun,* and some Scandinavian ones like *bathe* (both), *hærnes* (brains) and *drapen* (slaughtered) as well. *Martyr* is one of the few Latin loans that was borrowed into OE. The preposition *mid* means 'with' as in 'along with' or 'in company with' and the word *with* itself at this period still carried the sense of 'against' as in 'fight with'. Note how *writhe* is intransitive in modern English but monotransitive here, so that it would have to be translated with a mono-transitive verb like 'twisted'. A *pade* is more familiar to Scots speakers with the diminutive suffix {-ock} making *paddock* or *puddock*, 'frog' or 'toad'. Note how uncertainty in word division changed *a nadder* to *an adder*.

Inflectional morphology

The inflectional morphology has been greatly simplified since OE. Noun morphology is more like that of PDE. Some plurals are marked by a change of vowel: *men, fet* (feet). Most take an {-es} suffix, pronounced /əs/. *God* (goods), however, still takes no ending in the plural (like PDE invariant *sheep*). The third person plural personal pronouns (*hi, heom,* 'they, them') still have initial *h* as in OE. The verbs still have a plural inflection {-en} or {-on}: *namen, wæron*.

Syntax

The syntax retains evidence of the OE word order. The verb *hefden* (had) comes at the end of the subordinate clause. In the main clause, after the adverbial *ða* (then), the subject and the verb are inverted. The impersonal construction as in *me henged up* would have to be translated in PDE by using the passive *they were hung up*. The passive as we know it has not yet evolved. Note also that negatives are still cumulative. Two negatives are stronger than one and the three in *ne wæron næure nan martyrs* are quite emphatically negative.

Orthography and phonology

The orthography shows a number of changes since OE. The <qu> spelling shows French influence replacing the more phonetically representative OE <cw> in *cwearterne*, to give *quarterne*. <Th> spellings are beginning to appear alongside <ð> and <þ>. OE <f>, as in *hefed* (head) is occasionally being replaced by <u>, as in the alternative spelling of the same word *hæued*. This spelling suggests that /v/ is becoming recognised as a phoneme. (OE did not have this voiced fricative phoneme.) Later, the /v/ in this word is lost. This /v/-deletion has also happened in *hefden* (had). The vowels are still much the same as OE except that /y/ has been lost and the <y> spelling has become interchangeable with <i>. /w/ appears variously in this text as <w> and <uu>.

LATE MIDDLE ENGLISH (about 1300–about 1500)

As we move on into the fourteenth century, a new set of French loan words appear. These are more cultural, literary loan words. Great innovative writers like Chaucer were at work and many of them were translating texts from Latin and French, borrowing freely.

This passage was translated in 1387 by a Cornishman, John of Trevisa, from a Latin text written in the 1350s. It is interesting not only for the language itself, but also for what it has to say about what was known then about the history of the language, and for its dialectal and sociolinguistic comments. Read it aloud and you will find it quite easy to understand.

hy hadde fram þe beginning þre maner speche, Souþeron, Norþeron and Myddel speche in the mydel of þe
land as hy come of þre maner people of Germania.
Noþeles by commyxstion and mellyng, furst wiþ Danes
and afterward wiþ Normans, in menye þe contray
longage ys apeyred and som vse strange wlaffling,
chyteryng, harrying and garrying grisbitting . . . Chyl-
dern in scole, agenes þe vsage of al oþer nacions buþ
compelled for to leue here oune longage and for to
construe here lessons and here þinges in Freynsch . . .
also gentil men children buþ ytauȝt for to speke
Freynsche fram tyme at a buþ yrokked in here
cradel . . . and oplondysch men wol lykne hamself to
gentil men and fondeþ wiþ gret bysynes for to speke
Freynsche for to be more ytold of.

Vocabulary

There are a lot more French words here (*maner, people,
longage, apeyred* 'impaired', *strange, vsage, nacions, compelled, gentil*) and some Latin (*commyxstion* 'mixing', *construe*). Given the place of origin of the writer, you would not
expect a lot of Danish influence. Chaucer, in London was
using the Scandinavian *they*, although he still used *hyre* and
hem for *their* and *them*. As you move closer to the Danelaw,
you expect to find *they* and *their* alongside *hem* and, if you get
even closer, all three pronouns have initial *th-*.

Oplandish (uplandish or rural) seems to be used here with a
disparaging meaning. You will have no trouble in guessing
what *wlaffling, chyteryng, harrying and garrying grisbitting*
might mean.

Syntax

Word order is now very like PDE but note the absence of a
preposition in *maner speche*. Earlier, the relationship between

the two words could have been shown by a genitive inflection in *speche*. Now we use *of*. This text falls between two stools.

Inflectional morphology

Already, *children* shows the double plural. The verb morphology has {-eþ} marking the plural: *buþ* is {be} + {eþ} and the {y-} prefix in *ytauȝt*, *yrokked* and *ytolde* is a reduced form the OE {ge-} prefix found on past participles.

Orthography and phonology

The orthography shows that <y> and <i> are still interchangeable. This writer also obeys a spelling rule that says <v> must be used at the start of a word and <u> must be used in the middle. So *vsage* really starts with a vowel sound, /ʊ/, and *leue* has a /v/ sound.

Vowels were much more 'what you see is what you get'. So the <i> or <y> in *tyme*, *lykne* in pronounced [iː]; <e> in *þre*, *speke* is pronounced [eː] or [ɛː]; the <a> in *Danes* and *cradel* is still [aː]; <ou> in *Souþeron* is [uː] and <o> in *scole* is [oː]. From about 1400, this correspondence between spelling and sound began to break down as a result of the Great Vowel Shift which went on throughout the Early Modern English Period and is described more fully in chapter 9.

EARLY MODERN ENGLISH (about 1500–about 1700)

External history

Many exciting events were taking place in the late fifteenth century. The Renaissance was in full swing. The revival of classical learning, advances in science and the arts, exploration and the introduction of the printing press all had profound effects on the development of the language. The country was prosperous, and in such conditions the arts flourish. There was a new self-awareness about language and this makes the Early Modern Period a particularly interesting period to study, because people of the time were actually writing about their own language and books on spelling, pronunciation and grammar abound. In the second half of the period, dictionaries started being compiled, the first by Robert Cawdrey in 1604. Emigration to the New World began, the first step towards English becoming a world language.

Sample texts

Literary works by Early Modern English writers such as Shakespeare and Milton are readily available and there is an extended non-literary extract in the sample exam paper (question 13b) in Appendix II.

Vocabulary

There was an absolute explosion in the vocabulary of Early Modern English. With all the admiration for classical learning, there was a huge influx of Latin and Greek loan words, so many in fact that a dispute arose, known as the 'inkhorn controversy' because critics of excessive borrowing said all these new words 'smelt of the inkhorn'. In other words, these were words that people wrote, but nobody ever said them. Shakespeare sometimes has fun with people who like big words, as when Hamlet out-Osrics Osric (*Hamlet* V, ii) with words like *definement, perdition, inventorially, verity, extolment, infusion, semblable* and *umbrage* all confined in the space of a 78-word speech. Many new words were associated with the sciences: *anatomy, skeleton, virus.* Many Italian loans enlarged the vocabulary of the arts: *sonnet, soprano, madrigal.* The expansion of trade brought words from many countries: *potato* (Haitian via Spanish), *curry* (Tamil), *caravan* (Persian) and, *coffee* (Turkish) among them.

Syntax

There are still some older features of syntax. Questions and negatives can still be made without auxiliary verbs. *Sayest thou so? They go not.*

Thou is used between people in an intimate relationship and to address social inferiors, children and animals. *You* denotes formality, respect and/or lack of intimacy. Knowing this rule, you can appreciate some of the subtleties in Shakespeare. When, in *Twelfth Night* (III, ii), Sir Toby is trying to engineer a quarrel between Sir Andrew and Cesario, he tells Sir Andrew how to write a letter that will infuriate Cesario: *if thou thou'st him some thrice, it shall not be amiss.* Sir Toby is using the informal *thou* between intimate confederates, but for Sir Andrew to use it to Cesario would be inappropriate, disrespectful and insulting.

The perfect is formed using *be* + past participle with verbs of motion or change of state but *have* + past participle elsewhere.

> *He is not yet arriv'd* (Othello II, i)
> *He is much changed* (Othello V, i)

But

> *Thou hast enchanted her* (Othello I, ii)

The auxiliary verbs *do/did* and *gin/gan* are used as empty tense markers. So, in

> *Hark, hark the lark at heaven's gate sings*
> *And Phoebus gins arise*

Phoebus simply arises; there is no sense of 'beginning'. This *gins* is just saying 'present tense'.

Inflectional morphology

Nouns and pronouns (apart from *thou*) are much the same as in PDE. The verbs vary depending on the dialect but if we look at Shakespeare we find that a verb following *thou* takes the second person singular ending -(e)st and *he, she, it* sometimes take the old southern third person singular ending *-(e)th,* particularly in *doth* and *hath*, but the more frequent ending is the PDE *-s*. Plural verbs no longer have a plural inflection.

Orthography and phonology

Because of major changes in pronunciation, spelling, which tends to be conservative and pronunciation have got out of step. There is no longer the close relationship between sound and symbol that is found in OE. People started to agitate for spelling reform, but in order to find a new spelling system, they had to observe and describe what people actually say. Some of the Early Modern spelling reformers, known as the orthoepists, were more accurate and consistent than others, but what they had to say gives us a wealth of information about the pronunciation of their time. For an example of a suggested phonetic spelling system, see the passage in the sample exam question 13a (p. 213). This is by John Hart, one of the most reliable of the orthoepists. In his book, *A Methode or comfortable beginning for all vnlearned, whereby they may bee taught to read English, in a very short time, with pleasure*, he gave a description of how the various sounds were made and devises a system of one symbol to one sound, on much the same principle as the modern International Phonetic Alphabet. From this, we can work out that the great vowel shift had begun, because he used *Ei* to represent the word *I*. His spelling tells us that this had become a diphthong, rather than the earlier /i/ and that the quality was not quite the same as it is today, because the first part of the diphthong was a bit higher than in PDE. We can see he was still rhotic because /r/ appears in words such as *father*, *maker* and *lord* where most English speakers would not have /r/ now. You would think from the modern spelling of *almighty* that the <gh> must originally have represented a sound of some sort. Hart still had a sound which he represented as <h>. This was probably similar to a Scots /x/. His spellings of *huitʃ* (which) and *uas* (was) indicated that the two initial sounds were still different, just as they still are for most Scots speakers. However, the vowel in *sun* (son), *undr* and *kum* was the same as the vowel in *intu* and *kriu-si-feid*, just as it is in much of northern England still. Just think, in Shakespeare's time Macbeth would have seen his vision of the dagger and exclaimed: /kʊm let mi klʊtʃ ði/! The sound change, known as the FOOT/STRUT split, which gave us the /ʌ/ sound, must have taken place after Hart's time. Another orthoepist, John Wilkins, writing in 1668, has to invent an extra symbol to represent /ʌ/ and we can therefore deduce that the FOOT/STRUT split had taken place in the intervening century. Have a good look at the Hart passage in the exam question and you'll discover a few very odd things.

The Great Vowel Shift (p. 123) continued through the Early Modern English Period.

EIGHTEENTH- AND NINETEENTH-CENTURY ENGLISH

The interest in language which had produced reformers like Hart in the sixteenth century and Wilkins in the seventeenth century continued. Perhaps the best-known linguist of the seventeenth century is Samuel Johnson, the lexicographer. His *Dictionary of the English Language* still looks remarkably modern, with its typographically clear headword followed by the part of speech, the etymology (not always accurate), definitions and examples of the word in use. Some of his definitions are idiosyncratic, even biased, such as his definition of oats, 'a grain which in England is generally given to horses, but in Scotland supports the people'. Other definitions need a dictionary to understand them, like cough, 'a convulsion of the lungs, vellicated by some sharp serosity'. In spite of its weaknesses, Johnson's *Dictionary*, compiled in only seven years and published in 1755, set the standard for its time.

It was followed by a rash of 'pronouncing dictionaries' such as that of Thomas Spence in 1775 and John Walker's *Critical Pronouncing Dictionary* of 1791. These are useful from a vocabulary point of view and they are also invaluable for the historical phonologist. For example, both of these dictionaries tell us that there was no initial /h/ in the pronunciation of *hospital*.

As still happens today, dictionaries were regarded as 'authorities', and their spellings were taken to be correct. This played a large part in spelling becoming much more fixed and gave rise to the notions of 'correctness' in spelling that we still hold.

Prescriptivism and 'correctness' were in the air in the seventeenth century. A combination of political, social and intellectual factors coincided at that moment in history. The rationalists of the Enlightenment wanted to apply their scientific principles to language and get rid of irregularities and irrationalities, especially those found in regional and what they regarded as socially inferior dialects. The languages of Scotland, in particular, were in a vulnerable position. After the final defeat of the Jacobites at Culloden in 1746, a process of linguistic cleansing was initiated to eradicate the Gaelic language, a process which has only begun to be reversed in recent years. The Scots language, too, came under attack but, this time, as much from within as from without. It was a Scot, James Buchanan, who wrote: 'The people of North Britain seem, in general, to be almost at as great a loss for proper accent and just pronunciation as foreigners'.

The desire for regularity was not limited to spelling and pronunciation. This was also the period of prescriptive grammar books which banned the split infinitive (putting anything between *to* and an infinitive as in *to boldly go*) and, with the respect of the time for logic, decreed that negatives were no longer to be cumulative but that two negatives should henceforth make a positive. Grammar, up until this time, had meant Latin grammar. Nobody had bothered much with English grammar and, during the Enlightenment, all things Latin and Greek were held in enormous respect. Some observant and open-minded scholars, like Joseph Priestley (the discoverer of oxygen) noticed that Latin grammar did not quite fit English grammar, but they were in the minority. One of the best known and most influential of the grammarians was Robert Lowth. His *Short Introduction to English Grammar* of 1762 makes reference to current non-standard usage, but dismisses all such as mistakes and improper use. His was the pronouncement: 'Two negatives in English destroy one another, or are equivalent to an affirmative'. The criteria used by most grammarians of the time were reason, etymology and the grammar of Latin and Greek and they were quite determined to impose order.

All this prescriptivism did not mean that the language began to stagnate. The vocabulary was still increasing to accommodate all the technological advances. In England, there were sound changes such as the merger of /w/ and /ʍ/, and the loss of /r/ except before a vowel. The former is described by John Walker in his *Critical Pronouncing Dictionary*:

> H: this letter is often sunk after *w*, particularly in the capital, where we do not find the least distinction of sound between *while* and *wile*, *whet* and *wet*, *where* and wear. Trifling as this difference may appear at first sight, it tends greatly to weaken and empoverish the pronunciation, as well as sometimes to confound words of a very different meaning. The Saxons, as Dr Lowth observes, placed the *h* before the *w*, as *hwat*; and this is certainly its true place; for in the pronunciation of all words, beginning with *wh*, we ought to breathe forcibly before we pronounce the *w*, as if the words were written *hoo-at*, *hoo*-ile, &c. and then we shall avoid that feeble, cockney pronunciation, which is so disagreeable to a correct ear.

Walker also provides evidence for the beginnings of non-rhoticism:

> In England, and particularly in London, the *r* in *lard*, *bard*, *card*, *regard*, is pronounced so much in the throat

as to be little more than the middle or Italian *a*, lengthened into *baa*, *baad*, *caad*, *regaad*;

Nineteenth-century English does not present the modern reader with any major problems. There are one or two bits of
grammar that have since been lost, like the use of the pronoun
whom and the use of the subjunctive mood (p. 35) to suggest
doubt. Some words like *nice* and *gay* have changed in meaning. And, of course, changes in pronunciation are still going on
even now.

THE BALANCE OF EVIDENCE

The language detective looks for clues in a number of places.
In this chapter, we have gleaned a lot of evidence from
lexicographers and orthoepists and a bit of commonsense.
The fact that modern spelling does not correspond with
pronunciation in itself suggests that something has changed.
It is unlikely that *knee* would be spelt with a <k> if that <k>
spelling had not originally represented a sound. Sometimes,
naïve spellers give away clues about their speech. The extract
in exam question 13b is by a Londoner and there is evidence
here that h-dropping was already a feature of London speech.
Not only does he frequently write *his* as *ys* and *half* as *alff* but
he also puts <h> in surprising places, as in *blohyng* (blowing)
and *gohyng*. Other evidence can be gleaned from rhymes and
puns, but evidence from these sources must be approached
with great caution. Not all rhymes are exact and some puns
are absolutely groanworthy. Furthermore, we do not always
know whether a rhyme or pun was intentional. Shakespeare
could rhyme *winter wind* with *unkind* but what was the actual
vowel involved? People writing about their own language
would seem to be a reliable source of evidence but some
are more reliable than others. Whereas Hart is nearly always
consistent, Wilkins sometimes transcribes the same word in
different ways. For example, he transcribes *virgin* as *virgin* as
if it had a /g/ even although he uses *dz* to represent /dʒ/ in *Jesus*

and *judge*. It is unlikely that we will ever be able to reconstruct the history of the language in every detail but, by combining evidence from different sources and proceeding with caution, we can go quite a long way towards hearing the voices of the past.

AND MORE

Changes are still in progress. Some current changes and further examples of historical changes are covered in the chapter on Language change (Chapter 9).

FURTHER READING

Barber, C. (1964) *The Story of Language*, London: Pan. Goes right back to the earliest times. A fascinating, easy read.

Davis, N. (ed.) (1994) *Sweet's Anglo-Saxon Primer*, Oxford: Oxford University Press. The most accessible introduction to OE.

Baugh, A. C., Cable, T. (1993) *A History of the English Language*, London: Routledge. Highly readable and covers almost everything.

OE: Germanic, few loan words

ME: morphology and syntax undergo simplification; to Germanic vocabulary add Scandinavian influence (greatest nearer former Danelaw area), Norman French, Central French and Latin; GVS begins; highly variable orthography

EModE: vocabulary expands rapidly, GVS continues

18th and 19th centuries: prescriptive

6 REGIONAL VARIATION

> **Learning outcomes**
>
> - to know some of the ways in which dialects can differ
>
> - to have specific knowledge of South British Standard English and Scottish Standard English
>
> - to be ready to use that knowledge, independently, to describe other dialects

From the very beginning of OE, there have been regional variations. Today, as English has spread around the globe, there are international dialects of English such as American English, Indian English, Australian English and so on. Even within the British Isles, the range of dialectal variation is amazing.

The seeds of regional variation were sown right from the start with the different dialects of the Angles, the Saxons and the Jutes. From then on, a number of factors have caused dialects to develop differently. Sometimes it was a matter of external history, such as the influence of the Viking Danelaw on northern English and hence on Scots. Sometimes it seems to have been pure chance that one speech community chose to preserve a particular word or grammatical form and another speech community either changed it in some way or abandoned it for an alternative word or form. Changes are taking place all the time. (See Chapter 9.) Some of these changes become widespread; others stay comparatively localised.

Many of the examples in this chapter have been taken from

Scottish Standard English (SSE). This is both a social and a regional dialect in that it is the one most Scots aspire to use when they are speaking formally. It is what they learn in school and it is what most of them would regard as 'proper English'. Scots, by contrast, is considered by many to be a separate language, related to, but different from, either Scottish or English English. It can be very difficult to draw the dividing line between dialects and languages. Sometimes it has more to do with political boundaries than with linguistic boundaries.

One **dialect** differs from another in

- accent

- vocabulary

- syntax

- morphology.

ACCENT

It's easy enough to hear that people from different areas sound different, but it is much harder to describe exactly what the differences are. It helps if you have some idea of how the differences operate and if you build up a picture of the sound system of each accent. In order to do that, you must ask the following questions:

- What phonemes does the accent have? (Is there **phonemic variation?**)

- How are these phonemes actually pronounced? (Is there **realisational variation?**)

- Are there special rules about where the phonemes can occur? (Is there **phonotactic variation?**)

- What words are the phonemes used in? (Is there **lexical variation**?)

The accent described in Chapter 1 is RP. This is the high prestige accent of England. The majority of speakers in England, although they share many of the features of RP, will also have some of the accent features of the dialect of their own area. In Scotland, there are very few RP speakers and most Scottish speakers use a mixture of SSE and their own regional dialect, depending on their social status and on how formal they are being. Most of this chapter relates to differences between Scottish (and Northern Ireland) speakers and speakers from England in a very general way, so that you can easily find people on whom to test out the claims that this chapter makes.

Phonemic variation

As was explained in the chapter on phonetics and phonology (Chapter 1), you can construct a list of phonemes which includes all the sounds you need to distinguish between words. This list may differ for two different accents. This difference in the phonemic inventory is known as phonemic variation.

The SSE accent has two phonemes that RP does not have. Most SSE speakers distinguish between *which* and *witch* or *whales* and *Wales*. For them, a *wh* spelling represents a /ʍ/ sound. This is a voiceless /w/. If you do not have this phoneme yourself, try saying [hw], which is how some Scots actually pronounce it. Most Scots also distinguish between *loch* and *lock*. The represents a voiceless velar fricative, for which the symbol is /x/. It feels a bit like a /h/, made at the same place as /k/, only without the actual contact between the back of the tongue and the velum that /k/ has. So SSE has two extra phonemes which are not found in RP: /ʍ/ and /x/.

Conversely, SSE lacks three of RP's vowel phonemes. Words like *pull* and *pool*, *cot* and *caught*, *Sam* and *psalm* are minimal pairs for RP speakers but sound the same for most

Scots. SSE speakers lack the /ʊ/, /ɒ/ and /ɑ/ phonemes. Furthermore, where an RP speaker would pronounce /u/, /ɔ/ and /ɑ/ as long, but /ʊ/, /ɒ/ and /a/ as short, for SSE speakers all vowels are short. In RP, the vowels in *good* /gʊd/ and *food* /fud/ are not the same. So there is not even a clue in the spelling. This very unpredictability indicates that we are talking about phonemes. Unless you are a native RP speaker, you have no way of knowing which vowel an RP speaker would use.

If you are a Scot, ask an English person to say the following words for you:

> *Soon, foot, brood, crude, could, cool, wool, loose, lose*
> *Brought, pot, lot, soft, cost, prawn, sawn, cross, taught*
> *Father, cat, mass, charm, palm, Pam, salmon*

Can you hear the differences in the vowels? See if you can separate the *pull* words from the *pool* words, the *cot* words from the *caught* words and the *Sam* words from the *psalm* words. Ask your English informant if you are right. Keep working at it until you can hear the difference in the quality and the length of the vowels.

SSE speakers do sometimes use long vowels, but at least they follow a rule. This is known as the **Scots Vowel Length Rule** and it may be simply stated as follows: all Scots vowels are short except before voiced fricatives (/vðzʒ/), /r/, or root morpheme boundaries. (Like all good rules, this one has exceptions: it does not work with /ɪ/ or /ʌ/ and only works for some speakers with /ɛ/.) In a phonetic transcription, the symbol : denotes a long vowel. Note the difference in the SSE pronunciation of the following words:

> Bruce [brus] *bruise* [bruːz]; *grief* [grif] *grieve* [griːv]; *cat*
> [kat] *cart* [kaːrt]; *brood* [brud] *brewed* [bruːd].

Bruise and *grieve* have the vowel lengthened before voiced fricatives; *cart* has a long vowel before /r/; *brew(ed)* has a long vowel because the root ends with the vowel. This stays long even when an inflectional suffix is added.

If you are English, find a Scots speaker and check out their vowels. What words, in addition to the example above, could you use to test the Scots Vowel Length Rule?

Note that the long and short vowels in SSE are not separate phonemes. There are places where you know that the vowel had got to be long; otherwise, it will have to be short. Either there is a voiced fricative, an /r/ or a root morpheme boundary after the vowel, or there is not. The two places do not overlap and so you cannot get minimal pairs. So in SSE the vowel alone is never going to be enough to make the difference between two words. The difference already lies in what comes after the vowel. (Pairs like *brewed* and *brood* are not true minimal pairs because you are not comparing like with like.) So vowel length is allophonic in SSE; that is why square brackets are used when representing long and short vowels in SSE. Vowel length, however, is phonemic in RP because the vowel and the vowel alone makes the difference between words like *pull* and *pool*.

Examples of phonemic variation in other accents include the absence of an /ʌ/ phoneme in parts of the north of England, so that *luck* and *look* sound the same /lʊk/, and lack of the voiced affricate /dʒ/ in some Highland English speakers so that *cheers* and *jeers* sound the same.

Realisational variation

Whether you are Scottish or an RP speaker or a Cockney, you recognise that *bait* sounds quite different from *bit* and *beat* and *bet*. For all of us, therefore, the vowel in *bait* must have phoneme status. We all have that vowel in our phoneme inventory. However, we all pronounce that vowel phoneme in different ways. Scots have a monophthongal [e], RP speakers have a diphthong [eɪ] and Cockneys have [aɪ]. It is a matter of convention as to what the phoneme is called. Here it is called /e/. In other books, you may find that /eɪ/ is used instead. It really doesn't matter, so long as we all know which vowel phoneme we mean. Similarly, what is referred to here as the /o/

phoneme is pronounced, or realised, as a monophthong [o] in Scotland, as a diphthong [əʊ] in RP and [aʊ] in Cockney.

Modern RP speakers, SSE speakers and American speakers all have a phoneme which distinguishes *bat* from *bet*. It is referred to in this book as /a/ and modern RP speakers and SSE speakers pronounce it as [a] but very conservative RP speakers and Americans say it [æ] which is somewhere between [a] and [ɛ].

One of the best-known features of Cockney and Scots is the frequent use of the **glottal stop** [ʔ]. Cockneys and Scots have the /t/ phoneme but, except at the start of a stressed syllable, they may say it as a glottal stop. So, for them, [ʔ] is a possible allophone of the /t/ phoneme in words like *but* and *patter*.

Phonotactic variation

Phonotactic rules are concerned with what sounds can occur where. (Think of {tact-} from the Latin word for 'touch' as in *tactile* and *contact*. Phonotactic literally means what sounds are touching.) In the chapter on the history of English (Chapter 5), we deduced that, historically, words could begin with /kn/ as in knee. Over the years, this has changed so that a phonotactic rule can now has to be formulated to state that /kn/ is not permitted at the start of a syllable. A similar change has happened over most of England with the pronunciation of /r/. Originally, an *r* in the spelling was an indication that an /r/ was pronounced. Now, in RP, the position can be formalised in a phonotactic rule which states that /r/ is only pronounced at the onset of a syllable. So there is an /r/ in *rat* but not in *tar*. In Scotland, there is no such phonotactic rule. Where you get an *r* in the spelling, you get an /r/ in the pronunciation. This is a major difference between a Scottish and an English accent. The Scots are said to be **rhotic** and people who have the phonotactic constraint are described as **non-rhotic**.

A non-rhotic speaker does not have an /r/ in *car* but does have an /r/ in *carriage* because the /r/ occurs as the onset of the second syllable. This is known as **linking /r/**. It also works over word boundaries and so there would be an /r/ in *far and wide*. Again, the /r/ is pronounced as the start of the second syllable. Most non-rhotic speakers take this a step further put an /r/ in every time two vowels come together and say an /r/ in *drawing* /drɔrɪŋ/ and *law and order* /lɔrəndɔdə/. This /r/ where it does not really belong is called **intrusive /r/**.

Where would an RP speaker pronounce an /r/ in the following words and phrases?

> *Shorn, Sean, part, parrot, fear, far, afraid, perfect, per-ambulate, without fear or favour, India and America, rough and ready, through and through*

How would the RP speaker's pronunciation of these words and phrases differ from that of an SSE speaker?

Lexical variation

Sometimes, two accents have the same phonemes but the words they appear in may be different. Speakers in the north of England, like speakers in the south of England, distinguish between *psalm* and *Sam*. They have both /a/ and /ɑ/ in their phoneme inventory. They will agree that *father* is an /ɑ/ word, *cat* is an /a/ word and so on. But one of the easiest ways to distinguish between a speaker from the north of England and a speaker from the south is by their pronunciation of words like *bath*, *path*, *pass* etc. Where the southerner treats these as /ɑ/ words, the northern speaker has /a/.

Another example of lexical variation comes from America. Americans and RP speakers all have an /ɑ/ sound and an /e/ phoneme. They would agree that *father* is an /ɑ/ word and *bait* in an /e/ word. But what about tomato? Where RP speakers would put this in with their /ɑ/ words, Americans put it with their /e/ words /təmetə/.

VOCABULARY

Each part of the country has its own dialect words, from Thomas Hardy's Wessex – *grandfer* (grandfather), *stunpoll* (dimwit), *gallicrow* (scarecrow) and the highly onomatopoeic *zid* (saw) – to Shetland's *peedie* (small) *trow* (troll) and *norie* (puffin). Scots provides some good evidence of how vocabulary differences come about. Scots, not to be confused with SSE, is descended from northern Middle English which strongly showed the legacy of contact with the Danish Vikings. Both Scots and northern English have the word *bairn*. OE had two words for child, namely *cild* and *bearn* (*barn* in the northern dialect of OE). The Old Scandinavian word was *barnr*. In areas of Viking influence, this Old Scandinavian word reinforced the *b(e)arn/barnr* option and kept it alive in these parts of the country, although it died out elsewhere. Other Old Scandinavian words that are still used in Scots are *reek* (smoke), *lug* (ear) and, *brae* (hill). Later, during the wars between England and Scotland, the north of England began to look to London for its social, political, cultural and linguistic inspiration but Scotland held on to many of the Scandinavian words which the north of England lost. In the Orkneys, Shetland, Caithness and Sutherland, the legacy of the Norwegian Vikings is still evident.

Scotland shares with England many of the Norman French words associated with the period after the Norman Conquest but many French loans in Scotland reflect its own direct contact with French and should not be seen as having come via English. *Ashet* (serving dish) from *assiette*, *tassie* (drinking vessel) from *tasse*, *houlet* (owl) and *douce* (gentle, obedient) are all examples of words which were borrowed directly into Scots. Scottish trade with the Low Countries introduced such words as *dubs* (muddy puddles), *callant* (customer), *loun* (boy, young man), *dowp* (tail-end) and even *golf*.

At the same time as English writers were translating French and Latin works, Scots scholars were similarly employed, often working on the same texts. It is no wonder that many French and Latin words made their way independently into both Scots and English. Some, however, were borrowed exclusively into Scots and thereafter made their way into SSE, like the Latin words *domine* (headmaster) and *dux* (best pupil in the school). The fact that Scotland had, and still has, its own legal system meant that Latin legal terms were borrowed independently into Scots, like *compear*, and, although some of these words may have been borrowed into English legal language as well, the Scots ones sometimes have a different form, ending in {-ate} where equivalent English borrowings from Latin would have {-ated}. So we have Scots legal words like *examinate*, *dishabilitate* and *rememorate*.

DERIVATIONAL MORPHOLOGY

Affixes show some regional variation. The suffix {-ie} is often regarded in England as a childish diminutive but in Scotland, especially in the north-east, it is simply a colloquial, informal suffix used by people of all ages. Where English uses the prefix {be-}, Scots often prefers {a-}. So you get English *before*, *beside*, *below*, *behind* and Scots *afore*, *aside*, *ablow*, *ahint*. In Scots, adverbs are often formed by conversion from adjectives without the addition of {-ly} *Come quick!* or with {-s} *whiles* (sometimes).

SYNTAX AND IDIOM

Syntactic variation between dialects is rather harder to find than other differences. One feature which appears in a lot of regional dialects is the use of the double, or even triple negative, just as the usage was in Chaucer's time:

I never did nothing to nobody.

A feature of SSE and Scots is the use of *never* to refer to a single occasion:

I was in the bath, so I never answered the phone.

SSE speakers frequently reduce negatives like

He is not going.

to

He's not going.

whereas an English person would be more likely to say

He isn't going.

If you live in Scotland, a syntactic feature to listen for is the use of double modals found in Scots (but not SSE), particularly in central Scotland and the Borders:

We used to could see the boats coming in.
You'll no can dae that.

Most English dialects only allow one modal verb at a time.
    Another difference in the use of modals is the SSE speakers' preference for *can* where the English would be more inclined to use *may*.

Please can I go to the toilet? (I'm sure you can, *but you* must *wait until the end of the lecture.)*

Would you ever say *My hair needs washed* or *The cat needs fed*? If you would, you are almost certainly an SSE or Scots speaker. The south British Standard English equivalent would have to be *My hair needs washing* or *My hair needs to be washed*.
    SSE speakers use *the* in places where southern speakers would be unlikely to put it. *He goes to the church every Sunday* to an English person would have to mean a particular church whereas the Scottish speaker would be able to interpret

the sentence without thinking of any particular church building, but thinking of the institution.

If you listen to American speakers, you may hear some
differences in grammar and idiom. American English differs
from British English in its use of prepositions, for example.
You will hear Americans say: *I am going to visit with my sister*
where British speakers would say *I am going to visit my sister*.
An American would say *different than* where a British speaker
would say *different from*.

INFLECTIONAL MORPHOLOGY

Declension class words

In different dialects, members of minority classes sometimes
keep their older forms which may have been lost in south
British Standard English. So, in Scots, we get survival of forms
like *childer* and *shoon* (shoes). There is dialectal variation in
the pronouns. Some places, like Shetland and parts of Yorkshire, have kept the *thou* forms of the personal pronoun. Some
dialects which have lost the singular and plural contrast that
thou and *you* gave have got their contrast back by using new
local forms like *you-all* (Texas) and *yous* (Scotland and
Northern Ireland). In Scotland you may hear *wir* as the first
person plural possessive where you get *our* in other dialects.
Also in Scotland you may hear older speakers use the older
form *hit* rather than *it*. Scottish children may use *hit* to refer to
the person whose turn it is in a game such as *tig* (or *tag*,
depending on your dialect). The **reflexive pronouns** in Scots
are *masel, yersel, hissel, hersel, itsel, wirsels, yersels, thirsels*,
formed regularly from the possessive case of the personal
pronoun. The Scots forms are more regular than the English
reflexive pronouns. Wouldn't you agree?

Conjugation class words

Again, some of the dialectal variation shows retention of older forms, like {-en} on the Scots past participles *gotten, proven*. This is also the case in the Scots morphology of the verb *gae*. This is the Scots version of the English verb *go*. In Standard English and SSE, *go* is a suppletive verb, taking its past tense *went* from a completely different verb. Not so in Scots. The past tense of *gae* is *gaed*:

As I gaed doon the Canongate, I heard a lassie sing.

The regular Scots weak past tense is {-it}:

He biggit a hoose. (He built a house)

but the /d/ or /t/ allomorphs of the past tense morpheme in Scots are not uncommon. However, the /d/ allomorph is often devoiced to /t/. So, for example, the past tense of *turn* is likely to be pronounced [tʌrnt].

If you listen to a Scottish person telling a story, you may hear them use a narrative mood. This was much used in England in Chaucer's time but has survived to a greater extent in Scotland than in England:

And I says to her . . . and she says to me.

How is this different from an ordinary indicative present tense?

WORLD ENGLISHES

With so much regional variation within the small space of the British Isles, it is no wonder that there are major differences between the two varieties of English spoken on opposite sides of the Atlantic. American English (AmE) has its own features of accent, syntax, morphology, lexis and orthography. For example, we have already mentioned the realisational difference in that the /a/ phoneme is pronounced rather higher in AmE as [æ]. There are lots of vocabulary differences such as *sidewalk* (pavement), *potato chips* (crisps) or *vest* (waistcoat). Because the colonisation of America took place early, there are sometimes survivals from Early Modern English. This accounts for the lexical difference from RP in that they select a *Sam* vowel rather that a *psalm* vowel in words like *grass* and *bath*. This lexical difference, which we also find in northern English, came about because RP lengthened the vowels in these words but northern English and American English did not. Like SSE speakers, most Americans are rhotic, although there is some variation here depending on the date of colonisation and the region of Britain from which the colonists originated. The survival of dialect words in America can sometimes give clues as to where the original settlers come from. The American *scallion* (spring onion) came from the north of England. Of course, Britain was not the only source of American vocabulary and the multicultural ancestry of Americans can be heard in words like *rutabaga* (swede), *zucchini* (courgette), *delicatessen*, and *hamburger*.

Southern Hemisphere Englishes, like South African English and Australian English, share many of the later changes which occurred in RP. They are non-rhotic and have the /ɑ/ vowel in *grass, dance*, etc. They have, however, undergone their own changes in pronunciation and have enriched their vocabulary and idiom from the languages with which they have come into contact. For example, South African English has borrowed *aandblom* (evening flower), *dikkop* (blockhead) and *apartheid* from Afrikaans. Australian has borrowed *billabong, boomerang* and many names for animals (*kangaroo, koala, wombat*) from aboriginal languages.

For more information of the accents of Southern Hemisphere Englishes, see the sample essay in Appendix II.

THE 'BEST' ENGLISH

Just before we leave regional varieties of English and go on to
social varieties, this would be a good point to examine some of
your own ideas about what you, or other people might mean
by 'good English'. Is there any one pronunciation that is best?
RP, as we shall see in the next chapter, is associated with high
prestige and notions of correctness, but is it 'better' than any
other dialect?

One of the things that people criticise as being 'bad
English' is what they call 'lazy speech'. They would draw
your attention to the glottal stop as an example of sloppy,
lazy articulation, and perhaps you could call it that. However, ask the person who is calling the glottal stop 'lazy' to
say *postman* or *Christmas* or *cupboard* or *cardboard*. Do
they really say a /t/ in *postman* and *Christmas*, a /p/ in
cupboard or a /d/ in *cardboard*? Everybody, however carefully they think they articulate, makes allowances for surrounding sounds, anticipating what comes next or
simplifying difficult consonant clusters. 'Ah,' they say,
'but sloppy speakers make their words indistinct. They fail
to make the differences between words.' Well, RP is a high
prestige accent but RP speakers have lost any distinction
between *whales* and *Wales* and, for RP speakers *poor, pour
and paw* all sound the same, /pɔ/. An SSE speaker would
distinguish /pur/, /por/ and /pɔ/. In Britain, the high prestige
accent is non-rhotic. In America, the high prestige accent is
rhotic. Clearly, there is no way you can say that one accent
in better than another simply by looking at how efficient
they are at carrying information. Of course every dialect has
a few speakers who mumble and are justifiably called sloppy
speakers, but the dialect itself is not to blame.

When a non-standard speaker uses multiple negatives, there
is no confusion in the meaning. Multiple negation has a long
and excellent pedigree. Nobody is going to say that Chaucer's
English was bad. Again, each dialect has its own system of
grammar and some speakers and writers might make better
use of that system than others but, again, there is no one

dialect grammar which invariably expresses all things better than another.

On purely linguistic grounds, it cannot be said that any one dialect is the best. They are all equally suited to communication. If there remains any notion that one dialect is better than another, such a notion must be based on social rather than linguistic judgements.

FURTHER READING

Wells, J. C. (1982) *Accents of English*, Cambridge: Cambridge University Press
Giegerich, H. (1992) *English Phonology: an introduction*, Cambridge: Cambridge University Press.

Accent: phonemic variation, realisational variation, phonotactic variation, lexical variation;

Dialect = accent + vocabulary + syntax + morphology

Buzz words: rhotic, non-rhotic

7 SOCIAL VARIATION

Learning outcomes

- to identify and be able to discuss the effects of social class, age and gender on they way people speak

- to identify and and be able to discuss the way an individual's speech varies with situation

- to be aware of the conditions which encourage or restrict language change

Sociolinguists study how social factors affect the ways in which people use language. They may look at issues involving more than one language, such as which language multilingual speakers choose in any given social situation. They may even venture into the political arena with language planning, the place of official national languages and the support of minority languages.

The sociolinguistics of English alone covers many aspects of social interaction. Language does more than just convey what we mean: it conveys who we are or who we aspire to be. Have you got a 'telephone voice' or do you know someone who has? The fact that some people put on a 'posh' accent to answer the phone implies that there is a prestige accent. We can often get clues about a person's social class from the way they speak and the same person will vary their speech depending on the level of formality that the situation requires. If you think of the people you know with telephone voices, the chances are that most of them are women. The factors that affect the way we speak include social class, gender, age, formality level and the speakers with whom we are in contact.

SOCIAL CLASS

Most of us know what we mean by 'social class', but it is very difficult to define. In very general terms the higher the social class, the greater the status and power of the individual.

British speakers belonging to the highest social class speak British Standard English associated with the accent known as Received Pronunciation (RP). This is a Standard Dialect in that it has spread beyond the region of its origin (south-east England) and instead of being a regional dialect it has become a social dialect, associated with class rather than geography. The vocabulary, spelling, syntax and morphology of British Standard English are used in formal writing by all educated people throughout Britain, whatever their accent, but the use of British Standard English with an RP accent is a clear marker of class. The RP speaker gives very few clues as to geographical origin. RP speakers from Scotland sound much like RP speakers from Cornwall or Kent. Although RP speakers are beginning to use an increasing number of regional forms, as yet Standard English and RP are associated with high status and notions of 'correctness'.

Other Englishes have their own standards. American English is different from British English. Scotland, too, has its own standard. Although British Standard English with an RP accent is found at the very top of the social scale in Scotland, the middle classes use Scottish Standard English (SSE), described in Chapter 6. While a working-class speaker from Glasgow would sound completely different from a working class speaker from Dundee or Edinburgh, middle-class speakers from all over Scotland have a lot in common. When a Scottish parent or teacher says 'Talk properly!' they usually mean 'Use SSE!'

The further down the social scale a speaker is, the more regional features can be observed in their speech, particularly their accent, so that working-class speakers usually have a very strong regional accent and may use dialect words and grammar as well.

Remember that there is nothing that makes one dialect in itself any better than another. This is shown by the attitude to /r/ in Britain and America (New York). In Britain, the high prestige RP is non-rhotic (/r/ is not pronounced in *car*, *cart* etc.,) but, according to Labov (1978), in New York rhoticism is associated with upper-class speech. As Shakespeare remarked, 'There is nothing either good or bad but thinking makes it so.'

GENDER

Females are more likely to use standard forms than males. They are less likely to interrupt and they tend to use indirect, more polite forms of request. There are certain words which women are more likely to use than men, such as: *cute*, *gorgeous*, *divine*, and there are certain taboo words which most women avoid. The difference between male and female language was noted by the great Roman orator Cicero. His explanation was that 'women more easily preserve the ancient language unchanged because, not having the experience of the conversation of a lot of people, they always retain what they learned originally.' Modern evidence points to the complete opposite. Women who go out to work seem to use more standard speech than women who stay within their own communities. It has also been suggested that women use more standard forms because they are usually the members of the family who teach children to speak, but when mothers speak to their children, they are at their most informal and intimate, and these are the conditions where you would expect to find most non-standard forms. It is possible that there is a certain machismo attached to non-standard dialectal forms making them more likely to be used by men and avoided by women. It may be that women are more status-conscious than men and seek to gain status through language. It may be that women simply avoid aggressive and confrontational behaviour and this is reflected in their language. Whatever suggestions are put forward for the difference in linguistic behaviour between men and women, the real reasons are certain to be complex.

AGE

As a child becomes part of society, he or she is exposed to a greater range of speakers. At first children speak the same way as their family group or carers. As they are introduced to the educational system, they are subjected to two kinds of language. In the classroom they are exposed – some of them for the first time – to a standard language; in the playground, they speak with their peers, who may or may not come from a similar social background. Sometimes the gap between the local dialect as used in the playground and the standard language is great and the children become bidialectal. Moving into their teenage years, they may use language to indicate their membership of that particular age group. There are words that sound strange coming from an older person. Each generation has had its own vocabulary, long before the *fab*, *square* or *hip* of the 1960s, right up to the twenty-first century's *well cool* contributions. The frequent use of taboo words observed in some younger teenagers usually decreases as they reach their late teens. The workplace, especially if the speaker has aspirations towards upward mobility, brings an increase in the proportion of standard usage, but old age often brings a return to less formal, more regional speech.

Comparing the speech of different age groups can show how speech is changing over time. Older speakers may use words that are unknown to younger speakers. Younger speakers are introducing changes in grammar, vocabulary and pronunciation. For example, young speakers in Scotland are beginning to lose their /x/ and /ʍ/ phonemes. The relative pronoun *whom* (p. 30) has disappeared, even in writing, from the language of young people throughout Britain.

It is particularly difficult to get good data on the way

language changes with age. Most studies are what are called **apparent time** studies. People of various ages are interviewed and/or recorded and the data is compared. Unfortunately, this only tells us how people speak now; it does not tell us how the speech of the old people has changed. What is needed are more **real time** studies in which the same people are recorded at intervals over a period of many years, but for practical reasons these are rarely undertaken.

FORMALITY LEVEL

Wherever we fall between upper class and working class, most of us have the ability to vary the way we speak in that we can choose to use more or fewer regional features or we can speak more clearly and carefully on some occasions than on others. We speak in different registers or levels of formality. Answering the telephone at work requires a different register from telling a joke to your family.

People tend to be more careful when they are reading than when they are speaking. They are most careful when they are reading minimal pairs. Ask an informant to read pairs like *cap* and *cab* and the distinction between /p/ and /b/ will be made very clear. If the informant said *Put on your cap!* and *Call a cab!* the /p/ and /b/ might sound identical. Word lists are more carefully read than continuous prose. Spoken language too has a hierarchy of formality level. Things that are written to be read aloud, like lectures and sermons, usually avoid regional features. Interviewees usually do their best to speak Standard English. You probably hear more regional features in the playground than the classroom and more regional features in a pub than in an office.

ACCOMMODATION

Accommodation occurs when people vary the way they speak depending on the person they are speaking to. If you are speaking to someone further up the social scale, you usually play down your regional features. If the person you are speaking to shares a number of your regional features, you use more of them. This is **convergence**. Sometimes this can work the other way (**divergence**); if you want to distance yourself from the person you are speaking to, instead of converging, you exaggerate the difference. Accommodation can apply to more than just the number of regional features. It may involve speaking more loudly or more slowly. It may even cover the choice of topic of conversation so that the speakers have a subject of mutual interest. You might use short sentences to speak to children and non-native speakers. Although when speaking to a child you would use words of predominantly Anglo-Saxon origin, to a French, Spanish or Italian speaker you might be more inclined to use words of French or Latin origin.

THE OBSERVER'S PARADOX

As soon as you start to observe the way people speak, they speak differently. Often interviewers are middle class and the informant will accommodate upwards. Even whether or not the interviewer and informant are the same sex can affect the way they speak to each other. The presence of a microphone can elicit the 'telephone voice' or cause shyness. It is often a good idea to chat for a bit before switching the microphone on or to disregard the first few minutes of a recording. Ideally, the researcher should spend a lot of time getting to know the informant so that they are completely relaxed in each other's company. In practice, this is rarely possible.

SALIENCE

People do not change everything about their dialects to the same extent. There are some features of language that people pick out to adopt or avoid. The glottal stop [ʔ] is probably the feature that most people think of first. [ɪn] instead of [ɪŋ] in words like *runnin* and *thinkin* and h-dropping, as in *'e 'ad 'is 'at on 'is 'ead*, are also associated with lower class speech and informality. Features like this, which people notice, are called highly **salient**.

Variables

In sociolinguistic studies, the features that change with social class are called variables. Each variable has more than one variant. For example, [t] and [ʔ] are two variants of the same variable in words like *but* and *butter*. This particular variable is a marker in most varieties of British English: it changes with both social class and with formality level. There are other variables which give clues as to social class but which do not vary with formality. These are sociolinguistic **indicators**. Scottish speakers, although they are aware that the high prestige RP is non-rhotic, pronounce [r] in all positions, irrespective of the formality level.

Hypercorrection

In a study done in New York (Labov 1978), speakers from different social classes were observed using casual speech, careful speech, reading, reading word lists and reading minimal pairs. You will see that these are in ascending order of formality level. Their use of [r] after a vowel was the marker being used. All of the speakers had [r] in this position some of the time but, the upper class speakers were more rhotic that the lower class speakers. As the formality level increased, all the speakers became more rhotic. Again, knowing that [r] is a marker, this is what you would predict. Where it starts to get really interesting is the point at which the socially mobile lower middle class realise that their language is being tested, at which moment their use of [r] rises steeply and actually far outstrips the use of [r] by the upper middle class. They actually become posher than the poshest. This excessive use of a prestige variant is known as **hypercorrection**.

Social networks

In a very dense **social network**, everybody knows everybody else. A small village school might be a dense social network. The **plexity** of a social network is determined by the number of ways in which individuals are linked. The pupils and staff at the village school are linked though the school; they may also be neighbours; some of them may related to each other; they may play in the same brass band; hang about together outside school; go to the same church; go to the same football matches to support the same team. Within a dense, multiplex social network like this, there is little motivation for change. Where social networks are sparse, or of low **density**, then linguistic influences may be more diverse, presenting opportunities for change.

A sociolinguistic example

These data come from a study conducted in Livingston, a new town in Scotland, between Edinburgh and Glasgow. The original West Lothian inhabitants were joined by a large number of speakers from other areas, at first from Glasgow but afterwards from Edinburgh and, to a lesser extent from all over the UK and beyond. This population is highly mobile. The original dense, multiplex network that existed before the new town was built has been replaced by a sparser network of reduced plexity, providing ideal conditions for language change. One of the changes that is taking place is the intro-duction of a new variant of the TH-variable. The TH-variable, (as in *thing*), was found to have three main variants:

• the standard variant [θ] (*thing*)

- a new, fronted variant [f] (*fing*)

- [h] (hing) referred to as the traditional variant in the table below.

Older speakers never used the [f] variant and never used the [h] variant in word lists but used [h] frequently in informal conversation. For them, the TH-variable was definitely a salient feature and was operating as marker, varying with formality level. Primary school boys (PBs) and primary school girls (PGs), aged eleven, and secondary school boys (SBs) and girls (SGs), aged fifteen, provided the following results in a word list (WL) and in conversation. The figures are given as percentages of all occurrences of the variable.

	[f]		[θ]		[h]	
	WL	Conv.	WL	Conv.	WL	Conv.
PBs	33	15	65	51	2	19
PGs	16	9	82	82	2	9
SBs	58	16	42	17	–	67
SGs	18	10	82	50	–	40

As expected, girls show a greater use of the standard variant. The secondary boys, in conversation, actually use the [h] four times more often than either of the other forms whereas, for girls this variant never outnumbers the standard variant. The [h] variable is obviously stigmatised and is totally avoided in word lists by the older pupils. Even the primary children are quite sophisticated in their use of language and avoid [h] variants to a very great extent.

It is perhaps surprising to see that the new [f] variant appears in word lists. It is behaving more like an indicator than a marker. Its use actually decreases in informal speech with the increase in [h] variants. It seems that 15-year-old boys are the leaders of this change.

A few of the pupils did not use the [f] variant at all. Those who did use it, when questioned, admitted to using [f] but greatly underestimated how often they actually used it. They do not seem to regard it as a salient feature. Older inhabitants of the area, who has been brought up in the original settlement around which the new town was built, heard the [f] variable as highly salient. They frequently remarked on it as one of the big differences between the speech of new town children and their own speech. These older speakers quite often used the [h] variable in conversation, but, as you would expect, never in word lists.

FURTHER READING:

Holmes, Janet (2001) *An Introduction to Sociolinguistics*, Harlow: Longman. Highly readable.

Labov, W. (1978) *Sociolinguistic Patterns*, Oxford: Blackwell.

Robinson, C. (work in progress)

Trudgill, Peter (2000) *Sociolinguistics*, Harmondsworth: Penguin. Highly readable.

Social class, age gender, formality level

Buzz words: accommodation, variable, variant, salience

8 FUNCTIONAL VARIATION

Learning outcomes

- to understand how a text is constructed

- to recognise the characteristics of different functional varieties

- when writing, to be conscious of the purpose of the text and to work towards making the text more effective

As was observed in Chapter 7, the way we use language varies depending on the situation at the time. We take into consideration not just the formality level but also the person addressed; targetting the hearer or reader is essential if speech or writing is to be effective. This chapter looks at some other ways in which we tailor our written and spoken language so that it best fits the function for which it is intended. The function of language is primarily to communicate, but there are many different kinds of communication. Language can be used to inform, to persuade, to entertain, to transact, to warn and to perform a multitude of social functions.

Stylistics is a branch of language studies which looks at the techniques involved in making language work effectively. This chapter takes a quick look at two of the topics covered by stylistics before going on to a discussion of several genres.

GRAPHOLOGY

In order to function at all, a text must have structure. Some of the topics already covered in this book have been about structure: phonological structure, morphological structure, syntactic structure. Some genres are given also an external structure in the way they are written down. They have a distinctive **graphology**. When you look at a recipe, you know instantly what it is, with its list of ingredients set out in a column and the instructions written in imperative sentences below. You look at a newspaper article and you expect to see a headline in large heavy type, sometimes a by-line either giving the journalist's name or simply something vague like 'By our foreign correspondent', and then the body copy. The symbol of your star sign may direct you to the right part of a horoscope, but you know that Taurus always comes after Aries anyway. A report may have numbered sections and subsections. These external structures help you to recognise the type of text you are dealing with and help you to use the text by letting you know what to expect and where to find things, but that is still not enough. These external structures alone do not necessarily make a meaningful text. The text has got to be about something. It has to come together in some way which means that a text has also got to have an internal structure that links it all together. This is what is meant by **cohesion**.

COHESION

In order to communicate effectively, what is written or spoken must hang together. There are a number of devices that distinguish a coherent text from a random collection of sentences.

Reference

The use of pronouns is a linking device which relies on substitution. Pronouns usually refer to a person or thing mentioned earlier (an antecedent). This type of **reference** is **anaphoric**. If the pronoun comes before the person or thing it refers to, making the reader look forward in the text, it is **cataphoric** reference. Cataphoric reference can be used to create suspense. Which of the underlined words are anaphoric and which are cataphoric?

> *It was empty. <u>She</u> could not see the thing <u>which</u> <u>she</u> most feared. 'My sister's rat has escaped from <u>its</u> cage again!' Mary shrieked.*

Substitution

This involves the use of words like *do* and *so* to replace a much longer verb phrase or clause as in:

> *Do you understand all this? I hope so. (so = you under-stand all this)*
> *They all went home early and I did too. (did = went home early)*

Substitution can also be restricted to the nominal within the noun phrase as in

> *Have you got a pencil? This one is blunt.*

You will have noticed that these examples are anaphoric.

Ellipsis

Ellipsis means that something is missed out, but you can easily reconstruct the missing bit from the context.

Are you reading this carefully? Yes, I am.

Is this anaphoric or cataphoric?

Conjunction

Conjunction as a cohesive devise can be carried out using conjunctions, adverbs, noun phrases or prepositional phrases. They join text together in one of four ways: additive, adversative, temporal and causal. Which of these best describe the words underlined?

> <u>In the first place</u>, I slept in <u>because</u> my alarm didn't go off. <u>Then</u> I had to scrape the ice off the car <u>and</u> it wouldn't start. <u>Furthermore</u>, the battery was flat. <u>However</u>, I managed to get to work on time.

Lexical cohesion

Words themselves within a text can create lexical cohesion, holding the text together in a number of ways. A word may repeated or a synonym can be used. You can move from the general to the particular, or from the particular to the general:

> *Motorcycle enthusiasts will be delighted by the range of old British bikes on show. The Broughs, Nortons, Ariels, and Rudges are just some of the machines that will bring back memories to the more mature motorcyclist.*

The vocabulary of a text may hang together simply because a particular semantic field is appropriate to the topic or it may be that the use of one word triggers the use of another. In the last paragraph, the mention of *the general* made mention of *the particular* almost inevitable. Where you see the word *tense* you know that *past* and *present* are likely to crop up. These habitual partnerships are known as **collocations** and they, too, help to cement a text into a meaningful whole.

A VARIETY OF GENRES

Conversation

Language is, first and foremost, spoken. So let's have a look at some of the features of speech. You get a lot of instant information about speakers from your knowledge of socio-linguistics and dialectology. You can also hear from their tone of voice and deduce from their body language such things as whether they are nervous or relaxed, whether they are asserting a strongly held belief, making a tentative suggestion or perhaps even telling a lie.

With permission from the speakers, record an informal conversation and then try writing it down. Only when you try it will you begin to realise just how conversation works. The vocabulary is usually simple and colloquial. There will be pauses, pause fillers (*ums* and *ers*), false starts, ungrammatical sentences, sometimes self-corrections, all signs of **normal non-fluency**. Sometimes, a conversation, which seemed perfectly sensible when you were in the middle of it, makes little or no sense when written down, because the speakers may be carrying on more than one conversation at once or may be responding to non-verbal signals. You hear lots of **tags,** many of them with a strong regional character: *Know what I mean? Like. Innit?* People from Edinburgh use *Ken?* rather a lot. Without these characteristics of real conversation, people sound like characters from a Jane Austen novel. Another feature of conversation is turntaking. Notice how often this is achieved by the second person talking along with the first for a phrase or two before taking over. The switch from one speaker to another is not the clear-cut transition that it seems to be in plays and novels.

There are times when people do, in a way, speak from a script. Certain social occasions call for a form of words which people have come to expect and know how to respond to: introductions, asking a stranger for the time or for directions, welcoming guests, formal invitations. Can you think of other examples, either in face-to-face communication or on the telephone?

Written versus spoken

Taking things a stage further, some things are written down to be spoken later, for example speeches, sermons and lectures. You can usually hear that these have been written down first. What gives them away?

The grammar of written texts shows clauses linked by subordinating conjunctions (*because, if, when, where,* and so on) and relative pronouns (*who, whose, which, that*). In extempore speech, sentences are more likely to consist of single clauses or, if sentences are joined, the favourite conjunction is *and*. Written texts have a higher proportion of nouns. Speech makes more use of verbs. Compare

> *At weekends? Oh I like to go hillwalking and I em . . . ski quite a lot in winter. Yes . . . Even if there's no snow. We live quite near to a dry-ski slope and I go there. Mm . . . Not so much in summer. I like . . . prefer to get up to the hills in summer. You can make use of the longer hours of daylight, can't you? Use the long evenings and that.*

with the way that the speaker might write this down in a letter introducing himself to a penfriend:

> *My weekend hobbies include hillwalking in summer, when the longer hours of daylight are a great advantage, and skiing on snow or the local dry-ski slope in winter.*

Identify the noun phrases and the verb groups in each version. What do you find? Identify the content words in each. These are words like nouns, adjectives, adverbs and main verbs. Compare the proportion of content words with function words (pronouns, prepositions, articles, auxiliary verbs, tags).

You might like to look at some different types of written language. Here a few suggestions as to the kinds of texts which you might like to analyse along with some of the questions you will need to ask.

Scientific or technical language

The target reader is usually a fellow scientist and great deal of background knowledge is assumed. There is an expected order in which the information is given. There may be an introduction, which usually states what a particular piece of research is about and why it is needed and this is followed by the method, results, discussion and, if appropriate, recommendations. The grammar is characterised by impersonal constructions with many passive sentences. This is to make the writing look impartial. Reference is invariably anaphoric. The vocabulary is often highly technical and avoids any emotive words. Precision, accuracy and clarity are vital.

It may be of interest to compare a piece of genuine scientific writing with an advertisement which borrows from the scientific genre.

Horoscopes

What sort of person reads horoscopes? How much knowledge does this person bring to the text? Is there a particular vocabulary associated with horoscopes? How is it used to give the astrologer authority? Look at the modifiers, the subordinating conjunctions and the modal verbs. *If you look carefully, you are likely to find that the astrologer may be hedging her or his bets, at least while the moon is in Scorpio.* The use of the second person *you* effectively gives you the feeling that you are being spoken to personally. The frequent use of the imperative also makes you feel that the horoscope is a personal message and these imperatives and lots of modals help to increase the proportion of verbs to nouns, making the horoscope sound more like speech and therefore less formal and more intimate. There is also the distinctive graphology to help you find your star sign.

Newspapers

What makes a good headline? Watch out for puns, rhyme, assonance, alliteration and other forms of word play: SUPER CALLY GO BALLISTIC CELTIC ARE ATROCIOUS was a memorable headline relating to a football match. Are headlines always grammatically well-formed sentences? Is there always a by-line? Where is it and what form does it take? Compare a broadsheet with a tabloid. How does the layout differ? Examine the vocabulary. Is it emotive or neutral? Are there any cliches? What differences are there in sentence length and complexity, the length of noun phrases, the proportion of verbs? Is there much use of the passive? How long are the paragraphs? Why are there such differences and what effects do they produce? What readership do they appeal to?

Advertising

Advertising has some characteristic features. The product name is usually given prominence, rather like a headline. There is usually some body copy, often repeating the product name, and then there is the standing detail such as price and stockists. Increasingly, however, advertisers are doing their best to make advertisements look like anything and everything except advertisements. Some keep you guessing about the product name. Most of them mimic other forms of writing, like newspaper copy, scientific language, legal language or even literary fiction. Try to identify some advertisements with borrowed styles and, using the techniques practised in this chapter, assess how well these advertisements mirror the genres they seek to imitate.

LITERARY STYLISTICS

Everything in this chapter can be applied to the study of literature. In fact, your chosen course may cover literary stylistics with little reference to other forms of discourse except in so far as they are relevant to literature.

FURTHER READING

Jago, M. (1999) *Language and Style*, London: Hodder and Stoughton. A very interactive introduction to many different varieties.

Nunan, D. (1993) *Discourse Analysis*, Harmondsworth: Penguin. Absolutely no-nonsense elementary textbook with clear definitions and explanations.

Toolan, M. (1998) *Language in Literature*, London: Arnold. Covers much of the same ground but from a literary perspective. Another interactive book but rather more challenging than Jago.

Cohesion: reference, ellipsis, conjunction, substitution, lexical cohesion

Spoken vs. written

Graphology, vocabulary, sentence structure

Personal, impersonal, emotive, neutral

Inform, persuade, entertain, transact, warn

---

9 LANGUAGE CHANGE

Learning outcomes

- to appreciate some of the causes of language change

- to see how changes affect language systems

As the chapters on the history of English and regional, social and functional variation show (Chapters 5–8), language changes in all sorts of ways with time and place. But what brings about changes? An obvious answer is contact with other languages or dialects but, even without such external factors, language seems driven to evolve internally by at least two almost contradictory forces. On the one hand, speakers want to keep things simple: redundancies are got rid of, grammar rules are simplified, difficult consonant clusters are reduced. On the other hand, we want the language to carry as much information as possible and this can bring innovations or inhibit losses.

As well as changes taking place from within, or by contact with other languages or dialects (social or regional), changes can be brought about by various standardising forces, such as printing, social and political factors and the adoption of features associated with a prestige dialect; they can even, rarely, be brought about by grammarians setting out rules.

Still, there are a lot of changes for which no satisfactory cause has yet been suggested, and which, for the moment at least, must be put down to chance.

VOCABULARY

Vocabulary changes in response to internal or external forces.
Many new words are required to fill a gap in the language.
New philosophies, new systems of government, strange new
plants and animals and new inventions, all need names. So OE
started to borrow Latin loans in the semantic field of Christianity, like *martyr*, *psalm* and *shrine* as well as making new
words by compounding and affixation like *doomsday* and
gospel. The Norman Conquest brought the vocabulary of the
feudal system and the names of government officials. Exploration and trade introduced the English Language to tobacco,
potatoes, zebras and cockroaches (from Spanish *cucaracha*).
Scientific discoveries from Medieval times onwards have
spawned Latin and Greek formations like *television* and
deoxyribonucleic acid.

A number of loan words come in through travel and trade
but the long-term contact between language groups brought
about by conquest or colonisation provide the greatest
changes. Different types of relationships between the language
groups in contact affect the extent and type of borrowing.
They may also group around specific semantic fields; the
French influence on the vocabulary of food and fashion is a
clear example. Other borrowings appear to be more random
and new loans may be added alongside native words with the
same meaning. The usual course then is for one of them to
drop out of circulation, or for the words to diverge in some
way. We shall consider some very different scenarios of
languages in contact before going on to consider a few internal
changes.

Old Scandinavian

The Old Scandinavian languages, were like OE, members of
the Germanic family of languages and so they and OE already
had a large stock of words in common; this made borrowing particularly easy. Although the Vikings started off as

unwelcome raiders, the Danish kings in York ruled over Anglo-Saxons and Danes who seem to have lived peaceably as neighbours: trading, intermarrying and speaking to each other at the same social level. This is reflected in the everyday nature of the Scandinavian loan words which made their way into English: *knife, take, skin*. Sometimes, as in the case of *take*, the Old Scandinavian word *tacan* simply replaced the OE word *niman*. For a while, the two co-existed and when this redundancy came to be eliminated, it was only a matter of chance which one survived. Where an OE word and an Old Scandinavian word were very similar, the Old Scandinavian word helped to ensure the survival of its OE cognate. This accounts for the survival of *bearn,* in northern OE *barn*, reinforced by Old Scandinavian *barnr*, as the northern dialect word *bairn*. In other areas, chance determined that the other OE word, *cild*, would be the survivor as PDE *child*. An interesting interaction between the two languages can be seen in the word *dream*. In OE, this meant something like 'joy in the mead-hall', a sort of male bonding involving a lot of alcohol and boasting of martial exploits. The Old Scandinavian word *draumr* carried the meaning of the PDE word *dream*: we kept the OE form but adopted the Old Scandinavian meaning. The OE word for a plough was *sulh*. The word *plow* was a measure of land in OE but a plough in Old Scandinavian. We adopted the Scandinavian meaning and the OE word was lost.

Although borrowing from Old Scandinavian must have been going on in the OE period, loan words do not appear in OE writing. This may have had to do with the fact that the West Saxon dialect, centred around the ancient royal court of Winchester, and far removed from the Danelaw, was beginning to show signs of becoming the dominant dialect for writing. It may also be partly explained by the informal level of borrowing which may have made Old Scandinavian unsuitable for formal writing. Certainly, the extensive use of vocabulary of Old Scandinavian origin tends to be associated, at least in Older Scots poetry, with a low style of writing.

Norman and Central French

The social interaction between the Anglo-Saxons and the Normans was very different from the Anglo-Saxons' relationship with the Danes. There were no *franglais* chats over the garden fence. Numerically, the Normans were a small minority. Socially and politically, they were the dominant force. The Normans were either members of a social elite or soldiers garrisoning Norman strongholds, so that most of the linguistic interaction would have been between master and servant. If a Norman soldier retired and was given a patch of land, he would have been surrounded by OE-speaking peasantry and he would have been more likely to adopt the speech of his neighbours than to influence theirs. These factors concentrate Norman loan words in certain semantic fields such as those connected with power, government and social status (*crown, court, parliament, baron, noble, servant*). Loan words like *beef*, *mutton* and *pork* could have caused redundancy, but the Normans did the eating while the Anglo-Saxons did the herding of the native *cows, sheep* and *pigs* and so the Norman loans were restricted to the table.

Later loans from Central French came about because of English kings marrying French women and because of the popularity during the Middle Ages of all things French, including their manners and their literature. Many French works, including poems of courtly love, were translated into English and words were borrowed wholesale in the process.

Not surprisingly, French loans are generally associated with a higher, more literary style than Old Scandinavian loans.

Latin

Latin was in use throughout the Middle Ages as a lingua franca amongst educated people. It was commonly used in literary, religious and learned works. Borrowing was frequent in ME and during the Renaissance there was a huge influx of Latin words into English.

One of the results of these borrowings is that in PDE we have three tiers of style: Latin loans are associated with learned language, French is associated with the higher literary register and Old Scandinavian, with the native Anglo-Saxon, are at the everyday level of language.

Internal changes

New words have been created as the need has arisen, by the various methods described in Chapter 2. Old words have fallen out of use and died. Other words have changed their meaning. For example, the two OE words *cnaf* and *cniht* both meant 'young man'. You might like to look up the words *knave* and *knight* in the Oxford English Dictionary to trace the fall of one and the rise of the other and, at the same time, you could look up the words *nice* and *silly* as further examples of how meanings change.

Words are still changing. Many modern speakers are losing their awareness of any difference between *disinterested* (impartial, not having an interest) and *uninterested* (bored, not interested). Other words where distinctions are becoming blurred are *aggravate* and *irritate, persuade* and *convince*. One pair of words which are interchangeable for most people impinges on syntax: what is the difference between *fewer* and *less*? For all speakers, *fewer* can only be used with count nouns: *fewer tables, fewer people*. For conservative speakers, *less* can only be used with mass nouns: *less soup, less rain*. For these conservative speakers **less tables* and **less people* are ungrammatical. Some people are afraid that English is becoming less precise or less expressive. What do you think?

DERIVATIONAL MORPHOLOGY

Affixes which occurred with great frequency on borrowed words soon became recognised by English speakers as bits that could be detached and stuck on and these were added to the

stock of native affixes. So the borrowed negative prefix {in-}
joined the native {un-}, and the borrowed adjective-forming
{-ous} became an alternative to the native {-ful}. Other loan
affixes include {-tion}, {-al}, {-ity}, {dis-}, {mono-}, {anti-},
{ante-} and {-ology}. Roots, many of them bound, were also
added to the store of English morphemes. From Latin loans,
we have isolated the root {leg-}, from the Latin word for *law*,
{ped-} from the Latin for *foot* and so on, and we now treat
these as English bound morphemes and analyse them as such
in words like *legal, legitimate, legislate, pedestrian, pedal* and
millepede. Other roots which we can use productively in
English include:

Greek
anthrop-os a man (anthropology, anthropomorphic,
misanthropic)
mon-os alone, single (monosyllable, monotone, mono-
poly, monogamy)
gloss-a tongue (glossary, polyglot)
morph-e shape, form (morphology, amorphous, morph)
nekr-os dead body (necropolis, necrotic)
path-os suffering (pathetic, pathology, homeopathy,
sympathy)
phon-e voice (phonology, phonetics, telephone, symph-
ony)

Latin
ligare, ligatum bind (obligation, ligament, ligature)
loqui, locutus speak (eloquent, elocution, circumlocu-
tion, soliloquy)
pendere hang (depend, pendant, appendix)
specere, spectum behold (spectacles, inspect, conspicuous, spectacular)
terra earth (mediterranean, subterranean, inter, terrier,
territory)

As you might expect, as new morphemes are adopted, old ones
tend to become less productive. Many of the Latin and Greek

roots that were familiar to educated people only a generation ago have become little known as the classics are now seldom taught in school. So unless these roots are already highly productive in English like {tele-} or {video-}, they are unlikely to be used productively in the future. Roots are borrowed or invented much more readily than affixes and suffixes which are associated with particular parts of speech and are particularly resistant to innovation, although, as we have seen, change does occur even there.

PHONOLOGY

How can the phonology of a language be changed? Occasionally, external influences are involved, from another language or dialect, as in the development of voiced fricative phonemes. These resulted from contact with French. OE did not have voiced fricative phonemes. We can assume that the voiceless fricatives were voiced in voiced surroundings so that /f/ became [v] in words like *ofer*. However, this is a classic situation of an allophone since the /f/ phoneme was pronounced as [f] in voiceless contexts and [v] in voiced contexts and so they did not overlap and minimal pairs were impossible. Norman French did have voiced fricative phonemes, however, and once enough words containing voiced fricatives had been borrowed to introduce a number of minimal pairs (like *fine, vine*), voiced fricatives became established phonemes in English as well.

Old Scandinavian was responsible for many of the words with the initial consonants /sk/ and /k/. The equivalent (or cognate) words in OE were pronounced with a /ʃ/ and /tʃ/ respectively. It is because of Scandinavian influence that we now have pairs like *skirt ~ shirt* and *dyke ~ ditch*. In places like Scotland and north-east England where the Scandinavian influence was greater you find many more examples. What is the English equivalent of *kirk*, *birk* and *breeks*?

Usually, changes are phonetically conditioned. The way a phoneme is actually pronounced depends on the sounds round

about it and this can produce a number of changes by which
phonemes can be added, lost or restricted in the places where
they can occur.

Split

A phoneme which has been introduced, this time without any
external influence, is /ŋ/. In words like *sing* the final /g/ used to be
pronounced and the [ŋ] was simply the allophone of /n/ which
occurred before a velar stop. So *sin* and *sing* were heard as
different words because *sing* had a /g/. The fact that the /n/ was
actually pronounced as [ŋ] did not matter to the hearers any more
than you would worry whether *spangle* or *ink* were pronounced
with [n] or [ŋ]. It was the /g/ that they noticed. But the consonant
cluster was simplified and the /g/ was dropped. Only then could
[ŋ] appear in the same context as [n] and so minimal pairs like *sin*
/sɪn/ and *sing* /sɪŋ/ were possible and /ŋ/was elevated to the status
of a phoneme. So /n/ has split into /n/ and /ŋ/.

Merger

Simplification of the system has also occurred. In most dialects
the /x/ phoneme has been lost, either completely, as in *night*
and *bough* or by merger with /f/ as in *cough*. Where the /x/
phoneme has survived, as in Scots and SSE, the indications are
that it is now undergoing a merger with /k/ in SSE. The /ʍ/
phoneme has merged with /w/ in most dialects except in Scots
and SSE and again, a growing number of young SSE speakers
no longer have the /ʍ/ phoneme.

Phonotactic change

Simplifying the pronunciation, but creating new phonotactic
rules, there have been changes making /kn/ and /gn/ no longer
possible at the start of a syllable and making /mb/ unacceptable

at the end of a syllable. The spellings *knife*, *gnash* and *comb* reflect the earlier pronunciation.

Chain shift

The Great Vowel Shift (GVS) is an example of a chain shift. As can be seen from Figure 2.1, the long vowels all took part in a move which appears almost choreographed. Whether this change started with the high vowels diphthongising to leave a space and then each of the other vowels moved up in turn, or whether the low vowels started to move and pushed the others up out of the way is very much a matter of debate. Indeed, both pushing and pulling could have been going on simultaneously. What started the move in the first place is unknown. The GVS demonstrates how vowels space themselves out so as to maximise their distinctiveness.

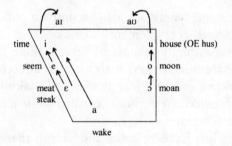

Figure 2.1   The Great Vowel Shift: sounds and spelling get out of step

INFLECTIONAL MORPHOLOGY

Because OE had a fixed word order, many of the OE inflectional endings were redundant anyway and towards the end of the OE period they were losing their distinctiveness. The vowels in the inflectional endings were being reduced to the indeterminate vowel *schwa* and some were being dropped altogether. This process continued into the Middle English period and beyond.

Analogy plays a large part in inflectional change. Many, many words have started taking an {-S} to mark the plural by analogy with General Class nouns: *stadiums, arenas, formulas, floods* (OE sg. *flod*; pl. *flod*), *books* (OE sg. *boc*, pl. *bec*). Within the general class nouns themselves, the {-as} inflection of the nominative and accusative plural was extended by analogy to the less common genitive and dative plural, so that in PDE, the {-S} plural is found throughout the plural. This (together with the loss of the dative {-e} inflection in the singular) has resulted in a change in the system: a merger or syncretism in the nominative, the accusative and the dative cases of nouns. Working alongside analogy is **levelling** through which the more unusual or extreme forms tend to disappear.

SYNTAX

To a great extent, syntax has also become simplified since OE. The subject–verb–(complement) word order is now used in main and subordinate clauses alike and there is no longer inversion of the subject and verb after an adverbial.

Getting rid of grammatical gender and making everything masculine, feminine or neuter according to its natural gender makes life a lot easier.

OE didn't just have singular and plural; there was also a dual number surviving in the first person and second person pronouns: *wit* (we two) and *we* (more than two); *git* (you two) and *ge* (you more than two). Another case of simplification.

The formation of the perfect has become simplified since EModE with *have* + past participle used for all verbs including intransitive and intensive verbs. However, the rule that says two negatives make a positive could be seen as a complication, as could the introduction of a rule requiring the presence of an auxilary verb in negatives and questions.

ME   *Go you?*
PDE   *Do you go?*

The introduction of the passive could be seen as a complication but it restores order and gets rid of all the idiomatic impersonal and passive-meaning constructions such as

> *Me henged bi the þumbes.* (They were hung by the thumbs.)

or

> *Oure corn is stolne.* (Our corn has been stolen.)

or

> *The house is abuilding.* (The house is being built.)

In modern English, we can now make a distinction between *Our corn is stolen* and *Our corn has been stolen*. In the first case we are in possession of someone else's corn. In the second case, someone else is in possession of our corn. There are remnants of the *is abuilding* form in PDE expressions like *There's nothing doing at the moment.*

FURTHER READING

Trask, L. R. (1994) *Language Change*, London: Routledge.

> See if you can identify changes going on in your dialect. What aspect of language is involved? Vocabulary and phonological examples should be easy to find. Would you regard these changes as increasing or decreasing the information bearing capacity of the language? Are mergers or splits involved?

10 LANGUAGE AND POETRY

Learning outcomes

- to be familiar with the structural conventions of English poetry

- to be sensitive to ways in which these conventions contribute to the effectiveness of a poem

This is not a chapter on literary criticism but it might give you some insights regarding the craftsmanship that goes into a work of literary art. Whatever the changing views of critics, for the English Language scholar at least the intentions of the author and the dialectal, social and historical linguistic contexts are of great interest.

If you are reading OE or Middle English texts, there is a sense of wonder in speaking words that someone wrote five hundred or a thousand years ago and in pronouncing them as closely as possible to the way that they would have been said. It is even more satisfying to get as close as possible to reconstructing what the author was trying to achieve in meaning and structure. Even since the time of Shakespeare and Milton, the language has changed so much that a knowledge of the history of English is needed to help you reconstruct rhymes and puns and appreciate subtleties of meaning. The chapters on history of English and language change (Chapters 5 and 9) will help you to turn back the clock and give you access to a millennium of English Literature.

The chapter on functional varieties (Chapter 8) is particularly relevant to the study of literary stylistics as they both seek to explore the techniques which must be perfected to produce literature of the highest calibre in any genre. Poetry, however, raises a few questions of its own.

LINES

What is the difference between poetry and prose? One major difference is that a great deal of poetry is written in lines (usually beginning with a capital letter) whereas prose is continuous. This is not simply a matter of graphology. In some old manuscripts, poems are written continuously to save space but it is still clear that these texts are poems because the lines and stanzas are demarcated in other ways, usually by repeating phoneme patterns, and stress and/or syllable patterns.

Line demarcation

OE poetry was alliterative. Each line had four stresses separated by variable numbers of unstressed syllables and there was no rhyme. In Middle English, there were varying degrees of sophistication and innovation. Rhyme became common. The end of a line is often marked by rhyme and repeating patterns of rhymes can be used to break a poem up into stanzas. Alternatives to rhyme are **assonance**, where the vowel stays the same but the consonants change (leaves, breeze, wreathe) or **consonance**, where the consonants stay the same but the vowels change (*seeds/sides, star/stir, tall/toil*). Even with these innovations, alliteration did not die out completely. There were some great medieval alliterative poems such as *Gawain and the Green Knight, The Pearl* and Langland's *Piers Plowman*. You will frequently see alliteration being used by modern poets.

Metre

Some poems in medieval times continued in the Anglo-Saxon vein, simply having four stresses per line and paying no attention to the number of unstressed syllables. This is known as **accentual verse**. Later, Coleridge reinvented this form for *Christabel*. Chaucer had a huge range of regular metrical patterns in his repertoire. He experimented with stanza forms and rhyme schemes. It was in the Middle Ages that regular patterns of stressed and unstressed syllables began to appear so that poets not only had to consider the number of stressed syllables but also had to worry about the number and arrangement of unstressed syllables. This is **accentual-syllabic verse**. In more modern times, poets have experimented with purely **syllabic verse**, keeping the same number of syllables per line but not having a fixed number of stresses. Haikus are examples of syllabic verse. Each haiku has seventeen syllables. Do you think syllabic poetry works well in English?

Accentual-syllabic verse is what we have come to expect when we think about metre. This depends on the perception of stressed and unstressed syllables. Most native speakers of English can feel the rhythm of a poem instinctively. If not, here are some suggestions to help you. As you speak, you give some words or parts of words more prominence than others. In *the cat sat on the mat*, which words would you stress? *Cat, sat, mat*. The other words are scampered over lightly. When you have words of more than one syllable, try to hear how the stress varies within the word. Listen to the two different ways of saying *conduct*.

> *His conduct was appalling.*
> *Did he conduct the orchestra?*

In the first sentence, the stress is on *con-* and in the second it is on *-duct*. In the word *orchestra* the main stress is on *or-* but the *-stra* is stressed compared with the middle syllable. The *-stra* would count as a stressed syllable in poetry because, although it is not fully stressed, it is more stressed that its neighbour: *orchestra* = tum-ti-tum.

English differs from many other languages in being a stress-timed language. This means that the time between each stressed syllable is roughly the same, unlike other languages like French where the length of a particular syllable is pretty much fixed, independently of what is round about it. In English, it takes almost the same time to say

/   /   /
One dead dog

as it takes to say

/ x x x /   x / x x
seventeen enormous elephants.

If you can read music, you will see that it is as if the stressed syllable were the first beat in the bar and it is held on to if it stands alone; any unstressed syllables are quavers, triplets or semiquavers as required. The more unstressed syllables you have, the quicker you must speak. In ordinary speech the foot is defined as the time from the onset of one stressed syllable to the onset of the next. In poetry, the unstressed and stressed syllables usually fall into set patterns known as iambic (x/), trochaic (/x), anapaestic (xx/) and dactylic (/xx). And depending on whether there are two, three, four, five or six feet in the line, the lines are called dimeters, trimeters, tetrameters, pentameters or hexameters.

Scan the following lines and describe them according to the number and type of feet. The first has been done for you.

1.   / x x   /x x   / x x   /
    Merrily, | *merrily* | *shall I live* | *now*
    / x x   / x   x   /   x   x /
    Under the | *blossom that* | *hangs on the* | *bow.*
                                (Shakespeare)

These lines are trochaic tetrameters. Note that a stressed monosyllable at the end of a line counts as a complete foot.

2. *Then the little Hiawatha*
   Learned of every bird the language.

(Longfellow)

3. *The ploughman homeward plods his weary way*
   And leaves the world to darkness and to me.

(Gray)

4. *I sprang to the saddle and Joris and he;*
   I galloped, he galloped, we galloped all three.
   'Good speed!' cried the watch, as the gate-bolts undrew;
   'Speed!' echoed the wall to us galloping through.

(Browning)

The good poet will chose a metre to suit the subject matter as in Browning's poem *How they Brought the Good News from Aix to Ghent*, where two unstressed syllables per foot hurry the reader on at a gallop. As Pope says in his *Essay on Criticism*,

The Sound must seem an Eccho to the Sense.

This poem is essential reading. It is full of useful advice to the poet and critic alike.

Listen to poetry being read. Usually, the normal sentence stresses and the poetic metre coincide, otherwise it could not be described as metrical at all. But where this is not the case, you can distinguish between two kinds of bad readers: the 'ti-tum ti-tum' readers who ignore what the words mean and those who read poetry as if it were prose, losing all feeling of the metre and the lines. The good reader will establish a background metre and, where the natural sentence stress differs from it, will create a tension between the two, to highlight the point that the poet is making. In *Anthem for Doomed Youth*, Owen sets a background iambic beat but breaks it with superb onomatopoeic effect, reflecting the rapidity of rifle fire, in

```
/   x  x  /  x x  /  x  /  x   /  x
```
Only the stuttering rifles' rapid rattle.

In the last line of the same poem, he creates the opposite effect by making the reader want to use more stressed syllables

```
x   /    /   /  x  / x   /  x   /
```
And each slow dusk a drawing-down of blinds.

This slows the line down to a funeral march. Note too how the alliteration of /d/ is a muffled drumbeat.

One of the curious things about metre is that feet like to come in pairs or dipodes. Try saying your favourite limerick and note the number of stresses per line:

There once was a student from Hull, (3)
Who thought English Language was dull. (3)
Said his tutor 'Gee whiz! (2)
It's the best thing there is. (2)
To dislike it is impossibull.' (3)

The first, second and last lines have three stresses or one and a half dipodes each. Note how you want to pause for a beat at the end of these lines. These pauses are silent stresses (marked hereafter by ^) turning a three-beat line into a four-beat line with two complete dipodes. Where the lines already consist of complete dipodes, like lines three and four, there is no silent stress and you move quickly on to the next line. Try clapping on the stresses and silent stresses:

```
  x   / x  x   / x  x   /     ^
```
There was a young lady from Ryde
```
  x /   x    x  / x x   /   ^
```
Who ate some green apples and died
```
  x /  x  x  / x
```
The apples fermented
```
x /   x  x / x
```
Inside the lamented

```
     x    / x x  /    x x  /    ^
```
Made cider inside her inside.

The iambic metre is closest to the most common pattern in prose speech and it is also the most commonly used in poetry. The bulk of Shakespeare's plays, Milton's *Paradise Lost* and the long poems of Alexander Pope are all written in iambic pentameters. Pentameters mean that there are two and a half dipodes and, therefore, where you get a pentameter, you also get a silent stress. If there is a grammatical break at the end of a line, marked by a comma, semicolon or stop, the silent stress also comes at the end of a line and then it aids in the line demarcation. This is **end-stopping**. It can also come elsewhere in the line. The pause created by a silent stress within a line is called a **caesura**. When the silent stress occurs other than at the end of the line, there is no longer any need for a silent beat at the end and the reader is free to proceed smoothly to the following line, with no pause at all, if that is what the grammar requires. The running on to the next line that this creates is called **enjambment**. End-stopping, caesura and enjambment are demonstrated very clearly in the opening lines of Milton's *Paradise Lost*:

> *Of man's first disobedience ^ and the fruit*
> *Of that forbidden tree, ^ whose mortal taste*
> *Brought death into the world and all our woe, ^*
> *With loss of Eden,^ till one greater man*
> *Restore us and regain the blissful seat, ^*
> *Sing, Heavenly Muse . . .*

The prepositional phrase *of that forbidden tree* wants to stay with the noun *fruit* which it modifies. The subject *mortal taste* wants to stay with the verb *brought*, just as *one greater man* goes with *restore*. Enjambment is necessary at the end of these lines to make sense of the grammar, and the lack of line-final silent stress makes this possible.

In short, when you look at a poem, look for a regular metrical pattern and if you find that the natural speech stress does not match, ask what effect the poet is trying to achieve. A move towards regularity, especially in final couplets, can coincide with a resolution in meaning, restoration of order or a coming to terms with emotion. As Othello gets more distraught, his iambics get more irregular.

THE STANZA

So far, alliteration, rhyme, assonance, consonance and repeating metrical patterns have been discussed in relation to the way they make up and mark out lines. These lines are often part of a larger structure, the stanza. Just as the lines are usually shown by the typology, so stanzas are often marked out by blank lines between stanzas. But, as with lines, the typology is usually supported with other signals such as a repeating pattern of line length and/or a recurring pattern of rhymes, giving a rhyme scheme. The usual way of describing a rhyme scheme is by using letters:

Full fathom five thy father lies;	a
Of his bones are coral made;	b
Those are pearls that were his eyes;	a
Nothing of him that doth fade,	b
But doth suffer a sea change	c
Into something rich and strange.	c
Sea-nymphs hourly ring his knell:	d
Hark, now I hear them – ding dong bell.	d

(Shakespeare *The Tempest*)

This stanza has a rhyme scheme *ababccdd*. It is always worth marking out the rhyme scheme of any poem to see whether there is some kind of pattern there. Also, look to see if there is any patterning of the metre. What combination of rhyme scheme and metre makes a limerick?

There are some special structures that you are likely to come across. Perhaps the most common is the **sonnet**. The sonnet form was borrowed from Italian poetry and consists of

14 iambic pentameters. Usually, the first eight lines form a sort of verse 'paragraph' called the octave and the last six form another 'paragraph' called the sestette. Often, the poet sets out a problem in the octave and finds an answer in the sestette. The original Italian sonnet had only two rhymes in the octave: *abba abba*, and Milton preferred this form. Shakespeare's sonnets have four rhymes in the octave: *abab cdcd*. The sestette usually has two or three rhymes and, although the patterns vary, the sonnet frequently ends in a rhyming couplet. If you are accustomed to reading sonnets by Milton and Shakespeare, you may have come to the conclusion that sonnets are always printed in a solid chunk and that they are a thing of the past. Not so. You can see from the rhyme schemes that there is potential for splitting sonnets up into smaller stanzas. Keep a lookout for sonnets in disguise. Wilfred Owen, for one, used the sonnet form.

You might like to take a look at Spenser's *The Faerie Queen*. This poem is written in what has become known as the Spenserian stanza, consisting of nine lines, rhyming *ababbcdcc*. The first eight lines are iambic pentameters, but the last line always contains an extra foot.

Many students are reluctant to believe that poets have put so much effort into rather formal structures, making poetry, in some respects, very much a craft. Modern poets do not feel bound by the poetic conventions of earlier centuries. Nevertheless, they are the inheritors of the poetic innovations of the past and there is not much in poetry that is entirely new. Some people think that **concrete poetry** (where the printed form of the poem reflects the meaning) was an invention of the twentieth century. Here is the first stanza of a poem called *Easter Wings* by George Herbert, written in the first half of the seventeenth century:

> *Lord, who createdst man in wealth and store*
> *Though foolishly he lost the same*
> *Decaying more and more*
> *Till he became*
> *Most poore,*

> *With thee*
> *O let me rise*
> *As larks, harmoniously,*
> *And sing this day thy victories.*
> *Then shall the fall further the flight in me.*

Not only is the sense suited to the line length but turn the poem on its side, and there is the shape of a pair of angel's wings.

GRAMMETRICS

In considering the language of poetry, the grammar of poetry has its own study, **grammetrics**, which is concerned with the way in which the sentences are constructed in relation to the lines, to the stanzas and even to the poem as a whole. (You may need occasionally to refer back Chapter 4.) Robert Browning's *Meeting at Night* shows the interaction between lines and syntax particularly well. Here is the first stanza:

> *The grey sea and the long black land;*
> *And the yellow half-moon large and low;*
> *And the startled little waves that leap*
> *In fiery ringlets from their sleep,*
> *As I gain the cove with pushing prow,*
> *And quench its speed i' the slushy sand.*

In the first line, you see two noun phrases. This is a line of two halves. The halves, linked by an *and*, are similar in that each has the definite article, a colour adjective and a head noun. The second differs from the first in that it has an extra adjective. The second line continues the pattern, consisting of a noun phrase, again with the definite article and a colour adjective. This time there is a bit of variation, though. The line begins with another *and*. What effect do *and*s have? Also, this line is all one syntactic unit with two alliterating adjectives coming after the noun they modify. Noun phrases are very static structures. Their use gets this poem off to a very slow start. The slowness, you will have noticed, is increased by the use of monosyllables and the number of heavy stresses. The ever increasing length of the noun phrases moves the reader along in gradually stretching strokes, becoming smoother as they go. The third line has the *and* again and now the third and fourth line form a complete constituent. In fact, these two lines form a big noun phrase. The headword is *waves* and there are two adjectives before this noun and a relative clause after the noun, modifying it. But, in spite of this being another noun phrase, we can really begin to feel the pace picking up. Why? In here we at last meet verbs. Although *startled* is doing the job of an adjective, it is really a past participle of a verb and *leap* is definitely a verb. The metre, too, has begun to dance along. These two lines are linked to the fifth by a different kind of conjunction, this time a subordinating conjunction. This link is tighter, smoother, without the staccato breathlessness of the repeated *and*. The fifth line keeps up the momentum with its verbs *gain* and the present participle *pushing* and the regular metre. With the sixth line, we are back to *and*. Looking at the stanza as a whole, there is something rather important missing between the first capital letter and the final stop. This stanza is punctuated as if it were a sentence, but is it? What is missing is a main verb. The lack of a main verb has the effect of making the stanza seem unfinished. The reader is left in suspense.

What we have here is powerful example of how the grammar can work together with the line structure and the metre to create atmosphere and to vary the pace. And the craftsmanship does not stop there. What about the phonology? Note how the alliteration ties half lines together. The /l/ sound is liquid and flowing. The voiceless plosive /p/ has force and effort behind it and the affricate /tʃ/ followed by the /s/ sounds in the last line are onomatopoeic. You really can hear a boat coming to a stop on a sandy beach.

It would be most unfair to leave you with this poem unfinished and so here is the second stanza for you to work on. Look at:

- the metre and any irregularities

- the rhyme scheme

- how the syntax fits the half-line, the line, or across lines

- the structure of each phrase

- nouns, verbs and adjectives

- conjunctions, or the lack of them

- the presence or absence of a main verb

- alliteration or onomatopoeia.

Ask yourself how each of these contributes to the atmosphere and the meaning.

> *Then a mile of warm sea-scented beach;*
> *Three fields to cross till a farm appears;*
> *A tap at the pane, the quick sharp scratch*
> *And the blue spurt of a lighted match,*
> *And a voice less loud, through its joys and fears,*
> *Than two hearts beating, each to each.*

FURTHER READING

Giegerich, H. (1992) *English Phonology: an introduction*, Cambridge: Cambridge University Press. This gives a theoretical account of stress, especially in chapter 9 section 2.
Leech, G. N. (1982) *A Linguistic Guide to English Poetry*, Harlow: Longman.

Iambic, trochaic, anapaestic, dactylic feet
Silent stress
Metrical stress vs natural speech stress
Grammar and lines
Sounds

True ease in writing comes from Art, not Chance,
As those move easiest who have learn'd to dance.
(Pope)

11 AND MORE

Learning outcome

● to appreciate the diversity of the subject

The foregoing chapters represent the main topics covered, in some way, in most English Language courses. It is highly unlikely that any one course will cover all these topics in the first year. Some may be reserved for second or later years. The content of courses may be influenced by the lecturers' research interests and if this is the case, you will be able to share the excitement of being at the forefront of knowledge. Such is the range and diversity of the subject that it has been impossible in a book of this length to cover all aspects. For example, in the chapter on vocabulary, the focus was on where words come from and how new words are created. This could have been taken further, by looking at some of the skills needed by an editor in order to compile a glossary or by a lexicographer in order to compile a dictionary.

The ideas that this book has introduced under the heading of functional variation (Chapter 8) might equally well have been introduced under the title of 'Stylistics' or 'Discourse analysis'. Stylistics and discourse analysis overlap to a very great extent: most books on stylistics tend to concentrate on literary work, while those on discourse analysis tend to be more involved with non-literary language. The tools used are, however, pretty much the same.

Closely related is the study of pragmatics, looking at what the speaker actually means rather than at the word or sentence meaning. The hearer may have to make inferences. Think of sentences like:

I'm over there!

If we restrict ourselves to sentence meaning, this sentence is clearly absurd, but you can create a context where it might make sense – what if the speaker was pointing to his or her car at the far side of the car park? How many contexts can you create for the following?

I told him to come today.
Go on!
It wasn't me!
I should have gone before I went.

In the first of these utterances, the meaning of *I* depends of the speaker. The meaning of *him* could change. *Come* suggests movement towards the place where the statement was made, wherever that is, and *today* is tomorrow's yesterday. What is going on here is a kind of linguistic 'pointing' known as **deixis**. This example contains **person deixis**, **spatial deixis** and **temporal deixis**. Unless the speaker and the hearer share the same context, the sentence cannot be reliably understood.

Sometimes we make **inferences** and understand more than is actually said. If you rush into a meeting breathlessly, and gasp, *Sorry, the bus didn't come*, everyone will make the inference that you normally travel by bus and you are providing a reason for your lateness. (Actually, you might live just round the corner and have slept in.)

The way we make demands is heavily dependent on factors that are outside the words themselves.

Would you mind leaving?
I'd like to be alone for a little while.
Push off!

Here we have a question, a declarative statement and an imperative, all saying the same thing. What factors determine the choice of words?

These are just a few of the questions asked by students of pragmatics.

English Language specialists can apply their knowledge to other practical fields. The development of language in children concerns parents, speech therapists and teachers at nursery and primary levels. Children learn to filter out phonemes at a very early age. If, as sometimes happens, they suffer from hearing problems in their early years, they may miss one or more phonemes from their inventory. It is important to help the child add that phoneme to his or her inventory as soon as possible. Knowing exactly how the sounds are made can help the carer, teacher or speech therapist understand why some sounds or combination of sounds are harder for children to say. A child who says [tat] rather than [kat] for *cat* may well be hearing the /k/ phoneme and have it stored away in an inventory of phonemes, but simply lacks the skill to cope with back consonants and this will right itself in time, usually without intervention. Stops generally come before the fricatives and /tʃ/ and /dʒ/ might not appear until the child is four or even later. There is considerable variation in the rate of development that can be considered normal. A knowledge of the phonology of English can help the therapist detect what is going on and decide whether action is appropriate. Another way in which a knowledge of English Language has helped speech therapists and their patients is in the recognition of, and respect for, the different phoneme inventories of different dialects.

(Teachers of English as a foreign language also benefit from being able to isolate the English phonemes that a student lacks. Now that you know a little phonology you can appreciate why there is no point in saying to a French student, who does not have an /ɪ/ phoneme, '/ʃɪp/ not /ʃip/'. They will hear you say '/ʃip/ not /ʃip/' and think what an unhelpful teacher you are.)

Once the sounds have been acquired, the child starts to form words and, by the age of eighteen months, many children use a vocabulary of about fifty words and understand many more. Between eighteen months and two years, the average child begins to combine nouns and verbs and then goes on to use prepositions to express spatial relationships and, although some children can understand passives by the time they are three, it is usually another year before they begin to produce passives themselves. The morphology of small children also takes time to develop. Plurals and past tenses are usually assigned to the majority classes, namely the {-S} plural and the {-D} past tense – so you get forms like *foots* and *goed*.

At the level of discourse, the child gradually builds up such skills as turn-taking in conversation, the ability to initiate or change a topic, awareness of the other person's level of knowledge and the ability to convey information clearly. These are skills which can be taught, when the child has reached the appropriate stage in its development, and it helps if the carer or teacher is aware of the processes at work. The ability to convey information effectively in writing and speech is not fully developed until the child is in secondary school and, it might be argued, not even then. Postgraduates and members of staff at Edinburgh University have the option of attending courses in presentation skills and writing skills and most of them would agree that improving communication skills is a lifelong mission.

Very little has been said in this book about English outside the British Isles. It is the majority first language in countries as diverse as Antigua and Papua New Guinea, Belize and St Kitts. In many other countries it a second language for the majority of the population. In the USA, a lot of work has been done recently on Black English and there are some interesting sociolinguistic parallels to be drawn between Black English and Scots regarding the status they are accorded in education and elsewhere.

Another topic which deserves a mention is the study of **pidgins** and **creoles**. A pidgin is a language which has no native speakers and which developed to allow communication among speakers of two or more languages. There is a very small vocabulary and a very simplified grammar. The phonology contains only those phonemes that the contributing languages have in common; the spelling is the rationalised. Tok Pisin, a language from Papua New Guinea, is one of several pidgins to which English was a contributing language. In Tok Pisin, all /f/s are replaced with /p/ and the word *fire* becomes *paia*. This words also reflects that fact that the accent of English used was non-rhotic. The information-bearing capacity of a pidgin is much reduced and it does not take long before the pidgin language itself begins to build up its vocabulary, characteristically by forming compounds. Can you translate the following extract telling you what to do and what not to do after an earthquake? Watch out for the tidal wave! (Answer on p. 146.)

- *Go lukluk sapos i gat paia.*

- *Lukluk sapos pawa i wok na wara i ran o nogat. Lukaut long ol pawa lain i pundaun long graun.*

- *Sapos pawa i no ran gut, mekim dai swis long numbawan bokis bilong pawa.*

- *No ken yusim telepon inap yu laik mekim wanpela ripot kwik.*

- *YU NO KEN GO WOKABAUT LONG OL RIP. Bikpela haiwara tru baimbai i mas kamap kwiktaim.*

True pidgins have no native speakers and, because they evolved for a limited range of uses such as trade they have limited semantic fields. But what happens when couples from different language groups, having only a pidgin in common, have children? The pidgin may be the children's first language. When there are a significant number of speakers who have the pidgin as their first language, the pidgin is then known as a creole and it rapidly develops to meet the complete range of contexts in which a first language is used. Not only does the vocabulary expand but grammatical features such as tense begin to be marked. Grammatical rules become regularised and generalised, and so on. The existence of creoles in multilingual societies can raise all kinds of political questions to do with status: what languages are to be taught officially in schools? Which are to appear on official documents and signs? Which may be used in a court of law?

This brings us to yet another issue: language planning. This covers questions of what languages are to be regarded as official state languages and related matters. What can be done to identify endangered languages or dialects and to promote their survival? Could Scots benefit from the kind of assistance that has been given to Welsh and Gaelic?

Finally, a few words on **onomastics**, the study of names. Placenames are interesting for a number of reasons. For one thing, they tend to be a bit like flies in amber; they can encapsulate fragments of geographical, social and linguistic history. They may contain very ancient elements, going back to pre-Saxon times. Celtic elements like *caer* (a fortified place) appear in Carlisle, Carstairs and Caernarvon. The Celtic *kil* or *cil* (church) appears in Kilmarnock and Kildare. The period of Roman occupation left behind *castra* (camp, fort) which appeared in the OE *Wiogoraceaster* (Worcester). From Anglo-Saxon times, the OE word *ceapan* (to trade or bargain) has given us the names of market towns such as Chepstow. As you would expect, words for settlements or homesteads often appear in place names; so we have *ham* in Birmingham, Nottingham and Cheltenham and *tun* in Livingston, Washington and Riccarton. We can tell where the main areas of Danish settlement were because there *-by* and *-thorp* replace the OE *-ham* and *-ton*. Later Latin elements, from the period of Christianisation, have given us *eccles-*, as in *ecclesiastic*, appearing in place names like Ecclesmachan and Ecclefechan, as well as *minster* in Warminster and Westminster.

The other element of settlement names is often a personal name. Livingston is the settlement of de Leving; Riccarton belonged to Richard: neither of them particularly Anglo-Saxon names. They give us some indication of the degree and location of French ownership of land. You see how this can begin to give clues about dialect and language contact. A word of warning! Although placenames remain remarkably stable, their spelling may have changed in misleading ways.

You should try to look back through old maps and documents to check the earliest spellings. You might even get as far as the Domesday Book or beyond. It is all too easy to be misled. For example, *burn* is a Scots word for stream. Whitburn is a town on the white stream. Blackburn is on the same river. It does not change colour. The *black-* in Blackburn is related to the OE word *bleac* meaning 'white' and from which we get the PDE word *bleach*. (A study of English Language even allows you to argue convincingly that black is white!) Knowing the meaning of *burn*, you might expect to find Burnwynd situated on a meandering stream, and indeed you would. But you would also find a long-established blacksmith's shop and, as a historical linguist, you might know that *burn the wind* was a medieval way of referring to a blacksmith (just think of the showers of sparks). Which do you think was the more likely source of the placename?

Personal names, like placenames, are interesting on their own account. They may be made up of OE elements like *ælf* (elf) *rede* (advice) as in Alfred. Or they may be loans, like Mary and Yvonne, reflecting religious or fashionable connections with other cultures. People who moved into other areas were often known there by the places they came from, so we get surnames like French, Fleming, Durham, Halifax and so on. This gives evidence of population movement. Medieval London documents giving lists of names at known dates show that the population shift is consistent with changes which start to appear in the dialect of London at these times. A particularly well-dated source of evidence for language change comes from Anglo-Saxon coins: they were renewed every few years and the moneyer had his name stamped on them. We know where the mints were, so we can take dialectal variation into account and changes in the spelling of a moneyer's name might be highly significant, but like all other language evidence, it has to be approached with caution and carefully weighed.

The study of English Language can lead down many paths and no first-year course can explore them all, but whatever aspects of English Language you study, you will find yourself listening and reading with a deeper understanding and interest.

Translation exercise

- Check for fire.

- Check your electricity and water supply. Look for fallen power lines.

- If the electricity supply is damaged, kill the switch at the main power box.

- Stay off the telephone except to report an emergency.

- DO NOT WALK ON THE REEF. A tidal wave is sure to come up by and by at great speed.

FURTHER READING

Nicolaisen, W. F. H. (1976) *Scottish Placenames*, London: Batsford. The standard of books on placenames on the market is extremely variable. Professor Nicolaisen is always scholarly and thought-provoking, but is very readable at the same time.

Crystal, D. (1995) *The Cambridge Encyclopedia of the English Language*, Cambridge: Cambridge University Press. Do not be put off by the heavy-sounding title. This really is a book to whet your appetite! It is full of illustrations and curious snippets of information. Just dipping into it will give you a lot of pleasure, but it is also a serious work of scholarship and is an essential reference book.

PART II
Study Skills in English Language

12 BE IN THE KNOW

You cannot settle down to study effectively unless you know what you are doing and why you are doing it. At all levels – what you are doing with your life, what you are doing at university, what you are doing in an English Language class – the more informed and aware you are, the better will be your motivation and your ability to study. This introduction aims to take some of the worry out of daily life. Do not be surprised to find, among the information on study skills, a number of hints on what might be described as life skills. For the time you are at university, the two are inextricably linked.

BE IN THE KNOW ABOUT YOUR SUBJECT

The class booklet

Most courses have a course booklet with essential information such as course content, reading lists, a timetable, what the assessment procedures are, whether or not you have to register for exams and if so, where and when. The course book may also tell you how essays and other written work should be presented. Always read the class booklet carefully, and refer to it from time to time, just to remind yourself of what you should be doing at any given point in the term.

The noticeboard

Find out where the class noticeboard is and keep a regular eye on it. Any changes to class times and locations will be posted there, sometimes at short notice. It is the place to look for tutorial lists, exam details and so on.

The departmental secretary

The departmental office may not be open to student enquiries all day. Find out when the secretary is available. This is where to go if, for instance, you miss a lecture and need the handout, if you want to double-check dates and places for exams, if you can't get hold of a particular lecturer, or if you change your address.

Computing support

Even if you are a complete technophobe, you must find out how to make the most of the available computing facilities. Increasingly, university departments insist that written work be done on a word processor. Some even ask for work to be submitted in an electronic form so that it may be scanned for plagiarism.

On a more positive note, a word processor makes editing and revising your work very much easier: you have the benefit of a spellchecker, and you can produce an attractive final copy, which will put the marker in a good mood. For larger pieces of work, such as dissertations and theses, the word processor may provide an appropriate layout.

There will almost certainly be courses on computing for new students and they are well worth going to, whether you are computer literate or a complete beginner. You will save a lot of time and effort if you find out how much your computer can do for you. The infinitely patient computing-support personnel are equally good at helping nervous beginners and the more adventurous, technically minded users.

The computer is also essential for gathering information from library catalogues and from the internet.

You will probably be given an e-mail address in your first

week. Check your e-mail frequently because this is how your tutors, lecturers or the departmental secretary will get in touch if they need to contact you urgently, and it will be appreciated by your tutor if you send an e-mail if you have to miss a class.

Before you even apply to a university, explore the websites of universities you might consider going to. They might help you decide which university to choose.

13 LEARNING: READING, ASSESSMENT AND SELF-DIRECTED LEARNING

Learning outcomes

- to know what to read

- to be able to find it

- to read effectively and efficiently

- to treat assessment as a learning opportunity

READING

Your lecturers will recommend reading to be done along with the lecture course. You will get the most out of the lectures and the reading if they keep pace with each other. Sometimes, a lecture course will follow a set textbook quite closely but there will almost certainly be additional reading so that you can broaden your knowledge of the subject and assess different points of view.

Your first task is to get hold of the book or article. There will be some texts that are recommended for purchase and, knowing that students are always short of money, lecturers will keep this list to a minimum. Watch the noticeboards for secondhand copies. If you are tempted to buy an old edition, check with your tutor that there have not been too many changes. Books that you do not have to buy will be in the library. Make sure that you are first in the queue – there are always more students than books. Right from the start, get to know your library and how it works. Get to know the shelf numbers where English Language books are kept (for instance: Dewey decimal system .4 . . .; Library of Congress system PE . . .). Practise using the online catalogue. It will tell you not only where to find books, but also whether they have been borrowed and when they are due back. If a book that you need has been borrowed, you may be able to recall it. Just ask at the service desk. There may be more than one place to find books. For example, there are the ordinary open shelves (or stacks) that make up most of the library but, in addition, especially when books are recommended for essays and there is likely to be a huge demand for them, books may be put in a special section of the library where they are on very short loans, say three hours at a time. If you have problems, the most valuable resource in a library is the librarian. Ask a member of the library staff for help.

The best academic writers, particularly those who are directing their writing towards first-year students, try very hard to keep their writing clear and easy to read. However, it is not always possible to express very complex ideas in very simple language. Furthermore, learning a new subject means learning all the terminology of that subject. Occasionally, some of the reading that you do will very dry and difficult. Persist. Gradually, you will build up your reading muscles to Olympic standards. This is yet another of the benefits of a university education; no act of parliament, company report or small print on a contract will daunt you after graduation.

The first half of this book will have given you some indication of the type of reading you will have to do. From it you can see that some topics are more readable that others, but none of it is exactly bedtime story stuff. It demands what is called 'active reading'. You really have to work and think along with the text. For this reason, do not underestimate how long a chapter will take and do not set yourself too big a chunk of reading in one sitting. Apart from the introductory chapter of each book, you are unlikely to be able to read a chapter straight through from beginning to end. Take a bit at a time. If there are exercises in the book you are reading, do the exercises for each section as you go along. If there are no exercises, set yourself some. Take notes. Try to rephrase the text in your own words as you do so. Occasionally, joint study sessions with other members of your tutorial group might be helpful. Together, you might make more sense of difficult passages, come up with good examples or be able to test each other.

The moment you sit down with a book, make sure you note down all the necessary bibliographical detail (see p. 179), including page numbers. Be sure to mark exact quotations in your notes. If you find something you may wish to quote word for word, make sure that you get every detail right, including the punctuation. If it contains what looks like an error, put [sic] after the error and then everyone will know that you are quoting accurately and the mistake is not yours. Much of your notetaking will consist of paraphrases or summaries of the text but often a passage from a book will spark off your own ideas. Make a note of the passage and write down your responses to the passage at once, or you will almost certainly forget what they were. Be sure that you make it very clear which notes are exact quotes, which are paraphrases and which are your own thoughts. (Use different colours of pen.) It is very easy, at a later date, to think an idea is your own when, in fact, you have picked it up in the course of your reading. Strangely, it is even possible to have an original idea and then to convince yourself that you read it somewhere.

Notes are an aid to learning, not a substitute for it. You should not just copy down words for future reference. Try to take notes in your own words. Before you can do that, you have to understand what you have read and that is the first step in learning. The physical act of writing something down will help to fix it in your mind. Also, you have to be selective and, in being selective, you begin to exercise your critical judgement. If you then take notes of your notes, you repeat these learning steps. If you are using your own book or a photocopy, you will probably use highlighter pen. Do not be tempted to use a highlighter or underlining as a way of not having to read something that you suspect is important but is too hard to understand. Make the effort then and there. If it is important enough to highlight, it is important enough to learn. Do not highlight indiscriminately or you will not be able to see the wood for the trees.

Only once you have done the recommended reading should you start looking for additional reading. The set books might make recommendations, or you could browse along the library shelves, or you could do a search on the library online catalogue. Subject searches are not always reliable. Sometimes keywords in the title can produce better results. This might produce such a wealth of material that you don't know where to start. A good guide is the number of times that a book or article is cited in other people's bibliographies. You will see from this which texts are important reading. If you need help, ask your tutor.

When you are browsing, use the contents page or abstract to identify useful and interesting bits and scan read to find the bits you want. Do not start at the beginning and try to work your way through. First make sure that the book or article has something to offer.

Get to know the major works of reference, such as the Oxford English Dictionary.

If you want to photocopy anything, you must obey the regulations on copyright displayed beside university photo-copying machines.

LEARNING BY ASSESSMENT

There are two kinds of assessment: formative and summative. The formative assessment counts towards your final mark but, even more importantly, it also provides you with the feedback you need to improve your performance and get the most out of the course. The summative assessment is the final test of what you have learned during the course.

The most usual ways of assessing student performance in English Language are essays, exercises and examinations.

There may be a small proportion of marks for tutorial participation. Most institutions now use continuous assessment, which means that classwork counts towards the final mark. In some departments, you may even be granted exemption from the degree examination if your coursework is of a very high standard.

Exams and essays usually give a very generous amount of choice. This practice can leave a large part of the course unexamined in any way. Some course organisers therefore prefer to set assignments which require short answers to questions covering a much greater proportion of the course curriculum. These assignments are not necessarily set under exam conditions but might take the place of a class exam. All the comments in Chapters 18 and 19 apply equally well to assignments.

Whatever form your assessed classwork takes, the marks are for your benefit as much as for the examiners' benefit. The class booklet should tell you what the marks really mean in terms of whether you have just passed, or passed well, or passed outstandingly. Go by what the class booklet says rather than by comparing yourself with other students. Some years seem to produce a larger number of good students than other years, but the marking criteria stay the same. Look at the markers' comments, good as well as bad, and try to see what makes a good English Language answer. If a few of you can get together and go over marked essays, exams or assignments, you will get a better picture of what markers are looking for.

SELF-DIRECTED LEARNING

Libraries are usually good places to work, if you can manage to ignore occasional, irritating whisperers. You are less likely to fidget and go off to do other things than you are at home. You are not going to be distracted by flatmates, visits to the fridge or your favourite television programme. If you are used to working in the library, you get into the habit of using it in breaks between classes, potentially useful time which can easily be frittered away.

If you live with other students, make sure that there are clear rules about not interrupting each others' study time. People who play very loud music at three in the morning before a flatmate's exam are not appreciated. Be considerate about your flatmates' exams and essay deadlines and make sure they do the same for you.

By now you will be aware of the length of time that you can work without a break. You are unlikely to be working effectively if you go for much more than an hour without a rest. You can keep up your concentration for longer if you vary your tasks. Read and notetake for a bit. Then do some practical exercises or test yourself in some other way before going back to reading again. Remember not to set yourself too much reading in one go.

Sit down to study with a realistic target in mind. Reward yourself (with a rest, a shower, a computer game, a chat with friends or a phone call) when you have achieved your goal.

Try to avoid working late at night. If you find that it is becoming a habit, revise your time management. If you do find yourself burning the midnight oil – and all students do from time to time – strong black coffee or other highly caffeinated drinks are not the answer. They may give you a short boost, but they will leave you even more tired and so you have another cup, and another. The result is that when you finally go to bed, you can't sleep and you will probably get a headache as well. Try herbal tea or a few deep breaths at an open window instead.

14 TIME MANAGEMENT

Time management is one of the transferable skills that employers value in a university graduate.

As you progressed through school, you will gradually have been given more and more responsibility for your own time management, but between school and university there is a great chasm. You were expected to get to school at the same time every morning and stay there and work until everybody went home. If you were not at a class, somebody wanted to know where you were. Homework was given in comparatively small regular amounts and woe betide you if it was not done.

At university, you may not have a class every day. You may start at nine in the morning, but you might not start until the afternoon. The strict routine of school disappears. You have to make sure you establish a good new routine. Bad time managers start getting up late, missing classes, working late to try to meet deadlines and end up feeling permanently tired, miserable and inadequate. Time management starts when the alarm clock goes off. You need to establish a daily routine.

You also need to keep an eye on the bigger time management picture. If you were a course organiser, how would you work out the deadline for handing in essays? You can't set an essay too early in the course because the work has not been covered. You want to hand marked essays back in time for students to learn from them before the exams. All course organisers think this way and so the deadlines for essays for all your subjects have a nasty habit of falling around the same time. It is no excuse to say: 'I had three essays to hand in for today. I haven't finished my English Language one. Please can I have an extension?' The time between the setting of the essay and the deadline is very generous, perhaps as much as five weeks. The time to get started is as soon as possible after the essay topics are given out. Furthermore, being quick off the mark means that you get to the library before all the books on the reading list disappear.

Some subjects you can swot up the week before exams and use flair or common sense to fill in the gaps. English Language is not one of them. It is not a difficult subject but it involves skills that have to be practised and built up over a period of time. If you keep up with lectures and tutorials and do the exercises that are set, you will find the exams are really not a problem.

You can improve your exam technique greatly by planning how much time you are going to spend on each question and sticking to it. You know the duration of the exam and you know the number of questions. Assuming that each question is worth the same number of marks, you simply divide the time equally among the questions. This may sound obvious, but it is amazing how many students make a mess of exams because they don't do it.

As you write an exam answer, you pick up marks very rapidly in the first ten or fifteen minutes of writing. After that, the rate at which you collect marks slows down and eventually you reach a plateau. There may even come a point when you end up exposing your ignorance instead of showing off your knowledge and your marks could begin to drop. So, obviously, it is better to start three questions than to finish two and leave one unstarted. Before you start practising for exams, work out how much time you can have for each question. Remember to allow for the time it takes to put your name on the paper and to fill in the other administrative details, question-reading time, thinking time and essay plan time. For essay-type answers, note the time at which you must start to draw each question to a close. Even if you have not completely finished when your time is up, move ruthlessly on to the next question. You may have time to go back and finish it later. Usually, each answer is written in a separate book, but, if this is not the case, leave a big space between answers so that you can go back and add any necessary finishing touches. If there are questions which are divided into sections, work out how much time you can afford to spend on each section and pace yourself accordingly. If you have practised on past papers, you may find that there are some questions you can do quite quickly. When it comes to the exam, do the quick ones first and divide up the time you have saved among the remaining questions.

If you have had to get a job in order to pay your way through university, keep your priorities clear. University comes first. When you start missing classes to go to work, something has gone wrong.

Finally, remember to plan some time for relaxation. If you deliberately leave time for having a bit of fun, then you will not be so tempted to let your relaxation time eat into your working time.

15 TUTORIALS, SEMINARS AND ORAL PRESENTATIONS

Learning outcomes

● to be able to make full use of all the different ways of teaching

● to make the most of your teachers

TUTORIALS

Tutorials are probably the most efficient and enjoyable way of learning. They usually consist of a small group of students and a tutor. Right from the beginning, get to know at least some of the people in your tutorial group. It can be a great help to go for coffee after a tutorial and talk about English Language with people who are at the same stage as you. It means that you will have people you know to sit next to in lectures. If for any reason you have to miss a lecture, it also means that you can borrow lecture notes easily.

The official aims of a tutorial are to reinforce lectures, to clarify any points in the lectures that you did not understand and to explore topics in more depth than can be attempted in lectures, perhaps moving on to related topics that were not covered in the lecture but which are still relevant to the course. To get the most out of a tutorial, you need to tell your tutor where your difficulties and interests lie.

Do not be afraid of asking something silly or giving a wrong answer. In tutorials, you are very unlikely be assessed on what you know (although you should clarify any criteria for assessment with your tutor). If tutors award a mark for tutorial performance at all (and not all courses have tutorial assessment) it will be based on attendance and participation. If you make a mistake in a tutorial, you and your tutor can get to the bottom of it and clear up any misunderstandings. Better to make a mistake there than in the exams or essays.

Attendance at tutorials is usually compulsory and if your attendance is poor, the tutor will be obliged to inform the course organiser and your director of studies or personal tutor. This is partly for academic reasons, to make sure you are not falling behind with your work. It is also for pastoral reasons, to make sure you are not ill or in some kind of difficulty. Please try to let your tutor know if you are going to be absent. Believe it or not, your tutor will worry about you. Because tutors are the members of university staff with whom students come into contact most frequently, they are often the first person that a student will consult about a non-academic problem.

Discussion plays a large part in tutorials, although first-year English Language tutorials are perhaps less discussion based than, say, English Literature tutorials. Each tutor has his or her own style of teaching, but you may well find that you spend a lot of time in your first year practising language skills, such as identifying and transcribing sounds or drawing trees for morphology and syntax. Your problem-solving skills will undoubtedly be extended. You will also look at speech and texts and, under your tutor's guidance, apply your growing knowledge of vocabulary and grammar to all the varieties of English associated with variation in time, place, purpose and social class.

Your tutor may well give you some clues about essay writing. If your tutor spends part of a tutorial giving a taught lesson rather than a discussion or practical session, look for structure. Can you spot possible section headings for an essay? For example, your tutor may divide a tutorial on regional variation into phonemic differences, realisational differences, phonotactic differences and lexical differences (p. 82ff). Make each of these into a section, add a short introductory paragraph and a short closing paragraph and you have a well-constructed essay on accents. If you are stuck with your essay, seek help from your tutor. Do not expect any help that would give you an unfair advantage, but your tutor may be able to discuss the topic with you in a very general way and sometimes the very act of explaining your difficulty to someone who understands can help you solve your problem yourself.

In the last tutorial before the exams, keep your ears tuned in for clues. Your tutor may be authorised to tell you a bit about the exam layout. You may go over old papers in the tutorial and be given hints on question spotting or hints on structuring answers. If the course has changed recently, past papers can put you in a complete panic by asking about things you have not covered, and your tutor will be able to reassure you. If the tutor does some exam revision with you, which topics are the focus of attention? After the exam, be sure to ask your tutor about any mistakes you have made if you cannot see for yourself how to put them right.

The better prepared you are for a tutorial, the more you will get out of it. Obviously, you will do any reading that the tutor has asked you to do and you should attempt any exercises that you are given as homework. It is not unusual for students to find some exercises very difficult at first. If that happens, do as much as you can and try to work out exactly where you are getting stuck. Let your tutor see your attempt, however pathetic it looks to you. Do not be embarrassed; you are not going to be the only one in the group who gets stuck. The tutor needs to know what areas of the course need extra consolidation and which bits are easy enough for you to revise on your own. If there is no set homework, make sure that you have understood the lectures and the recommended reading that goes with them. Tell the tutor about the bits that are not clear.

If you have any special needs, tell your tutors if there is anything they can do to help. For example, if you are partially deaf and need to lip read, suggest to the tutor that you sit where you can see the tutor's face clearly, in good lighting, and ask the tutor to help by speaking clearly. If the tutor lapses and starts talking to the blackboard, a quick reminder will not cause any offence and would actually be appreciated by the tutor.

SEMINARS

Between the full-scale large lecture and the small, intimate tutorial lies the seminar. It is a rather vague term because different teachers approach seminars in different ways. Some treat them as large tutorials and others treat them as small lectures. There should be more opportunity for questions and comments in a seminar, so come well prepared in order to contribute but, because it is a larger gathering, you must also let other people speak and take care not to monopolise the teacher's time. Do not expect the same level of individual attention that you get in tutorials.

ORAL PRESENTATIONS

Some tutors expect students to give oral presentations in tutorials. It is not very likely that this will happen at the start of first year. By the time you have to give a talk, you will be familiar with your subject and friendly with the other members of the tutorial group, who are all going to have to go through the same torment.

Your oral presentation will be based on a written paper, produced with all the skills you would use for writing an essay. Many tutors will be quite content if you simply read from your written paper. Your fellow students, on the other hand, will be bored to tears. So:

• Try to keep your voice interested and interesting.

• Be sufficiently well prepared so that your nose is not always buried in your paper.

- Mark the important points in your paper (probably topic sentences) with a highlighter pen, so that you can find your way at a glance.

- As you speak, watch your fellow students and make eye contact with them and the tutor.

- Smile.

- Invite questions and comments and be prepared to deal with them.

- Do not be afraid to admit that you do not have all the answers.

- With your tutor's permission, make use of any appropriate audio-visual aids (whiteboard, overhead projector, computer screen, recordings).

- Provide a handout if you think it would be useful.

16 LECTURES

First-year English Language classes can be quite large. A certain amount of noise is inevitable, particularly during the winter term when everybody seems to have coughs and colds. Coughs, inexplicably, get worse during lectures. Therefore, it is a good idea to arrive in good time and get a seat quite near the front where there is less chance of being distracted and you will be able to hear. If the lecturer is inaudible or if the visual aids are not visible, let the lecturer know at once. If you have a hearing problem consult the university's special needs advisor. If you have a motor or visual problem and cannot take notes, ask the lecturer if you can use a tape-recorder. Nobody should use tape-recorders without permission.

Lecturing styles vary quite a lot and so you must be able to adapt your note-taking and listening. Most lecturers provide a course outline in the class booklet and it is a good idea to take a look at this and get a general picture of where the lecturers are heading. Some lecturers follow a published book (sometimes their own). If there is no suitable book to refer to, you may well get a handout at the lecture or handouts may be collected in a class booklet. If there is such a class booklet make sure you take it with you. If the lecturer sticks closely to the handout, it might be enough just to make marginal notes on it. If there is no handout, or if the handout is extra to the content of the lecture, be sure to take notes. You may think you will remember it all but you won't. A good lecturer will have planned the lecture and it will have a structure. In fact, even although the lecturer may sound quite spontaneous, the lecture should have been constructed in sections and paragraphs like a well-thought-out essay. The lecturer may tell you the gameplan at the start of the lecture. Try to structure your notes accordingly. Use bullet points and numbers where possible. Use a different coloured pen to highlight key terms and VIPs (Very Important Points). This will help with exam revision. You would be very exceptional if your concentration did not lapse occasionally in lectures but train yourself to wake up rapidly if the lecturer gives any VIP signals.

Not all lecturers are charismatic and riveting. You may have to make a big effort to stop your attention from wandering. On these occasions, you could try active rather than passive listening. Imagine you are in a radio discussion programme and you are going to have to respond to what the lecturer is saying. What can you agree with? What would you question? What stimulates you to think in fresh directions? Not only will this game help to keep you awake but it will also help you to take good notes.

At the end of a lecture, there will probably be a short time for questions. Do not be afraid to ask. If, however, you cannot bring yourself to speak in front of a large audience, have a private word with the lecturer afterwards. Questions are useful feedback for lecturers, who need to know whether their lectures are pitched at the right level.

Always take a look over your lecture notes, and make sense of them, the same night, while the lecture is still fresh in your mind; if there is recommended reading to do, do it as soon as possible after the lecture. You might like to revise your lecture notes with a friend, in the hope that your absent moments do not coincide and that, if one of you has a gap in your notes, the other can supply the deficiency. By the same token, if you miss a lecture, borrow notes for the same lecture from at least two people.

Make a special effort to get to the last lecture of every lecture block or module. This is when you might pick up hints about exam questions.

17 ESSAYS AND DISSERTATIONS

Learning outcomes

● to treat essay writing as a chance to learn

● to understand the process of writing an essay

● to anticipate what the markers are looking for

● to produce a polished piece of work

● to write in an appropriate way for the subject

You did not get as far as considering university entrance without having gained some skill in writing, but learning to write well is a lifelong task. During your time at university, you will be expected to polish your formal writing style and adapt to the particular conventions of the subject you are writing about.

At university, you will be assessed primarily on what you write, and that is inseparable from how you write, because it does not matter how much you know if you cannot get that knowledge down on paper in a way that makes sense to the reader.

Make the most of available technology. Many university departments insist on the use of word processors for essays and you should take advantage of computing courses for new students.

WHY WRITE ESSAYS?

The obvious answer is 'to prove that you have learnt something'. That, however, is not the only or the best answer. If you tackle your essays in the right way, you will find that they are, in fact, a very important part of the learning process. It is only when you try to explain things in a totally clear and unambiguous way that you begin to expose little gaps in your understanding. So you have to go off and consolidate your learning. More encouragingly, you may find that, as you arrange your ideas, you make connections that you had not seen before. You are putting what you have learnt to work and gaining confidence in handling your new knowledge. The more effort you put into an essay, the more you will benefit.

Essay writing at university level demands knowledge of the conventions of academic discourse and especially of the way of writing accepted within the academic circle of your particular subject. All academic discourse demands attention to detail, not just in the facts and theories you present but also in the manner of presentation. A consistent level of formality is required and an impersonal style where the writer does not get in the way of the subject. Vocabulary and grammar have to be carefully checked to make sure there is no possibility of misunderstandings. Bibliographies and sources have to be cited. You are handling complicated ideas and having to express them clearly. In short, you are becoming expert in the transferable skills of gathering, selecting, organising and communicating information.

Essay writing is a very important part of the learning process.

FIRST READ THE QUESTION

More good students get bad marks because they have misread the question than for any other reason. There are certain recognisable types: *Discuss . . .*, *Compare and contrast . . .*, *Describe . . .*, *Analyse . . .*, etc. Think about it. Make sure you undertake the activity asked for.

Everything you write must be relevant to the question. If you include irrelevancies, they will not gain marks and they will even lose marks by taking up space that should have been used for answering the question. Word limits on essays are based on the assumption that every word is necessary and to the point. Lecturers think very, very hard about the exact wording of questions. If you are in any doubt what an essay question means, do not be afraid to ask whoever set it.

Choose your question wisely. With experience, you will discover the kind of question you are best at.

THE WRITING PROCESS

Writing is not a single big task. It is a lot of little tasks:

- collecting data

- finding a structure

- making a draft

- polishing

- preparing for submission

- proof-reading.

COLLECTING DATA

Sources

Most of the information you need will have been covered in lectures and reinforced in tutorials. A good essay, however, shows signs of additional reading which has obviously been well understood and used appropriately.

Make sure you can use libraries to the best advantage. Find

your way around online catalogues. If you can't find what you are looking for, or don't even know where to start looking, ask the librarians. They will be happy to tell you what is available. You can surf the Net for sources including databases which are available to higher education institutions within the UK, such as AHDS (Arts and Humanities Data Services). For a list of internet sources, see Winship and McNab (1998). A word of warning: especially in the early stages, you can be overwhelmed with sources of information and you may not yet know enough to be selective. This is why your teachers provide recommended reading lists. Use them.

Taking notes for essays

When taking notes, keep the exact wording of the essay title in front of you. Constantly ask yourself 'How does what I'm reading relate to the title?' Noting down your initial reactions to what you are reading can be a good way of getting into the actual writing of your essay.

Since academic writing demands that you provide proper bibliographies listing all the works you have consulted, it is particularly important that you record all the necessary bibliographic details (see p. 179). If you take something off the internet, make sure you record the name of the website with the date you accessed it.

Only if you are using your own photocopies are highlighter pens acceptable! Remember not to break copyright rules when you are photocopying. The rules should be clearly displayed near the university photocopiers. If in doubt, ask a librarian.

FINDING A STRUCTURE

Students are usually surprised at how much importance markers attach to the structure of essays. Anybody can regurgitate facts. That is not what essay writing is about. Markers are looking for the ability to put the facts to work. Different subjects place a slightly different emphasis on the way facts are manipulated but, in general, you are expected to construct some kind of argument. In this context, argument does not necessarily mean anything confrontational. It simply means that your essay should have a thread running through it.

Sometimes the wording of an essay title suggests a structure: *Discuss the effects of sex, age, social class and formality level on the use of the glottal stop in Scottish speakers.* This rather suggests a brief introduction, four main, discursive, fact-presenting paragraphs and a brief closing paragraph.

If no obvious structure suggests itself, experiment with different ways of writing an essay plan.

Some people use mind maps. Put the core idea down on the middle of a bit of paper and let other ideas branch off. These secondary ideas might generate their own branches. Little clusters start to form. These might each form a section or paragraph of your argument. Do not worry if the same idea crops up in two places but ask yourself if that produces a possible link between sections.

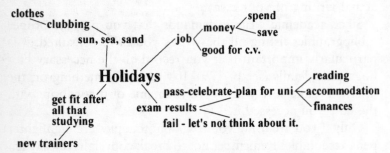

Figure 3.1 A mind map: paragraphs, sub-paragraphs
and links between paragraphs are beginning to form

You might prefer a more linear plan, like a flow chart, or you might try grouping related facts, for example listing pros and cons, and identifying major themes. These strategies may uncover such possible orders as: a logical progression as a proof unfolds, a chronological progression moving linearly backwards or forwards in time, a spatial structure, dealing with different geographic or topographic areas, a movement from the general to the particular, perhaps stating a hypothesis and testing it on specific examples, or moving from the particular to the general, constructing a hypothesis from the evidence you have set out.

If no plan emerges, do not despair. Sometimes the act of writing brings the necessary insights. Get started on free writing. To do this, just write as fast as you can, without stopping to think or lifting your pen, for at least three minutes. It doesn't matter if you write nonsense. At least you have something on paper to expand, reorder and improve.

If you still cannot see a way of making all the data hang together as a whole instead of a jumble of facts, seek help from your tutor.

FIRST DRAFT

The first sentence is always the hardest. A good way of tackling the opening paragraph is to put the question into your own words or say what you understand by it and prepare your reader for the way you are going to answer it. It will help your reader to understand your essay if you give an overview of where you are heading. You could state your objectives or list the main issues you intend to deal with (in the order that they appear in your essay) or say briefly what you intend to explain or discuss. In this opening paragraph, you want to get the reader on your side by arousing interest.

If you are having difficulty getting started, remember that you do not have to start at the beginning. Some of the ideas that you have jotted down whilst reading and note-taking can be written out to form a series of nuclei around which you can build up your text. Then you can fit them into your planned structure. If you prefer to write straight on to a word processor, a smaller window can be less intimidating than a huge blank screen waiting to be filled.

If the words still will not come, try talking. Explain what you are trying to write to your flatmate, your cat or your bathroom wall. Write it down exactly as you said it.

Ideas are like buses – either none come or they all come at once. So when you have plenty of ideas, just concentrate on getting them all down. Whether you use a word processor or pen and paper, just enjoy the experience. Worry about spelling, grammar and the exact words later. An essay which overflows with ideas and has to be refined is better than one that has to be padded out.

Stay flexible. What you write may give you new inspiration. You may find connections you had not noticed before and you may need to revise your essay plan a bit. It is very easy to move chunks of text around on your word processor; experimenting with structure is not a problem. However, when you move text around, make sure that the seams don't show. Read it over to check that the section you have moved fits into its new surroundings.

The final paragraph should not introduce any new material or any new ideas. An old recipe for an essay structure is:

- say what you are going to say

- say it

- say that you have said it.

This plan has been sneered at as over-simplified but there is a lot of sense in it. In particular, you will not go far wrong if your closing paragraph briefly restates the question and says how you have answered it. If you cannot show in your final paragraph that you have answered the question, perhaps you should ask yourself if you really have done so.

Make absolutely sure that everything you say is relevant. If necessary, point out why it is relevant. By now the essay title ought to be engraved on your heart. But just check again to make sure you have not lost sight of it. Is your essay a discussion, a comparison, or evidence in support of a hypothesis? Is that what was asked for?

Check for the following trademarks of woolly thinking:

- When you use a pronoun, can you identify the exact word or phrase it replaces? *This, these, that* and *those* are real danger words. After a long ramble, students often write, 'This means . . .' when it is not at all clear what 'this' was. An extreme example is afforded by a letter to the DHSS: *I have not received any money from you. I have six children. Can you tell me why this is?*

- Be careful when starting a sentence with an *-ing* word or an *-ed* word. Make sure that the *-ing* or *-ed* word really does relate to the subject of the sentence or you could end up with nonsense like

  > *Walking down the main street, the parish church comes into view.*
  > *Covered in a warm travelling rug, the coach bore him off into the night.*

- Make absolutely certain that you have not missed out any steps in your argument.

By now you should really be confident that you understand your material and it is time to pass that understanding on to your reader as effectively as possible.

POLISHING

Effective communication is what makes good writers stand out. When you are writing essays, it is very easy to fall into the trap of thinking that this is between you and the page and you forget that a real person is going to have to read it and perhaps even enjoy it. Consider your reader.

Your reader is a well-informed academic who is going to take you and your essay seriously. The style is therefore formal. This does not mean that it has to be long-winded. It is very often the people who understand their subject best who can explain it most simply and directly. Those who have only half a grasp of what they are talking about are the ones who are most likely to dress up their shallow knowledge in dense language. They think they know what they want to say, but when it comes to putting it down on paper, the words won't come because they have not thought everything through. If you can say what you mean with absolute clarity, you will demonstrate your knowledge effectively. Look at every single sentence you write and ask yourself whether it is crystal clear. Trying to achieve this clarity will often expose a lack of understanding on your part and that is what makes essay writing such a good learning opportunity. You expose the gaps and work on them. Do not be tempted to fudge.

Murphy's Law of Writing: if your readers can misunderstand something they will. (And Murphy was an optimist.)

PREPARING FOR SUBMISSION

A departmental stylesheet telling you how to set your work out is often given in a class booklet. If not, here are a few suggestions:

1. Make sure your type face is big enough:
   - You could use 8 pt for footnotes at a pinch.
   - but 10 pt is just about the limit that older eyes can read comfortably for any length of time.
   - 12 pt is easy on the eye (especially for ageing academics who have a lot of essays to read).
2. A page with plenty of white space is more attractive than a black, solid block of text. Make sure you use big margins so that the marker can write helpful comments. Separate your paragraphs with a blank line instead of indenting.
3. If you are quoting more than one line of poetry, or more than three lines of prose, you should indent the quotation:
   > It is not enough to attain a degree of precision which a person reading in good faith can understand, but it

is necessary to attain if possible to a degree of precision which a person reading in bad faith cannot misunderstand.

(James Stephen 1890)

This may be combined with a change of size:

> Moreover, you need to choose the right words in order that you may make your meaning clear not only to your reader but also to yourself. The first requisite for any writer is to know just what meaning he wants to convey, and it is only by clothing his thoughts in words that he can think at all.
>
> (Sir Ernest Gowers)

Note that, when indentation is used for a quotation, there are no quotation marks.

4. Imaginative use of fonts may help to make a point but for the main body of your text avoid weird and wonderful fonts.

FOOTNOTES OR ENDNOTES

Your departmental stylesheet may give a ruling on this. If not, try to do whatever helps the reader. It is an irritation constantly having to flick to the end of a text. On the other hand, too many footnotes on a page can make for a very ugly appearance. For a few short notes which are important to the understanding of the text, the foot of the page is best. If they are copious and more for form than necessity, tuck them away at the end.

REFERENCES AND BIBLIOGRAPHIES

The purpose of references and bibliographies is to enable your readers to find for themselves the material to which you have referred. They may want to check your accuracy or, more positively, they may be stimulated by your writing to go and find out more. Whenever you are picking up another author's idea, even if you are not using the exact words, it is usual to use the author's surname, the date of publication and the page number in brackets (Wiseman 1999: p. 999) after the citation or, if the author's name is part of your text, just bracket the date and the page number: Wiseman (1999: 999) is a fictitious example. If an author has more than one publication of the same date, these are designated 1999a and 1999b, etc. Proper referencing is essential if you are not to be accused of plagiarism.

Plagiarism, whether intentional or unintentional, is a form of cheating with which universities are very concerned and they are increasingly vigilant to ensure that students do not copy work, whether from other students, published sources or the internet. There are even computer programs designed to detect plagiarism. Of course you will present and discuss other people's ideas, opinions and theories in your essay, but you must say where you found them and you must be very careful not to claim them as your own original thoughts.

Bibliographies are a horrible chore, but the task can be made a lot easier if you note all the necessary information right from the very beginning of your research. It is soul-destroying chasing round libraries looking for things like page numbers and place of publication when the rest of the job is done.

The perfectionist will ensure that the latest editions of books are consulted wherever possible but, if you cannot get hold of the most recent edition, list in your bibliography the one that you actually referred to.

If you are referring to a website, you must make sure that you give enough information to make sure that a reader could access the same site. Give the date on which you accessed it in case the site has been updated since you used it.

The exact formats for bibliographies vary greatly and attention should be paid to where full stops, commas and so on are used. If there is no set format, these are possible options:

Author, A. N. (1995) *Book Title in Italics*, Place: Publisher.
Author, A. N. (1996a) 'Article title without capitals,' *Italicised Journal Name*, 10 (3): 1–55.
Author, A. N. (1996b) 'An essay in a book,' in S. Cribble (ed.) *Book Title*, Place: Publisher.

PROOF-READING

Always proof-read on a hard copy. You will need to proof-read several times because you cannot do all the tasks at once.

Stage one

Take a break. It is very difficult to proof-read your own work and the more of a distance you can put between writing and rereading the better.

Stage two

Read for general sense and good communication. Read it out loud. Are there any bits that are unclear, get your tongue in a twist or sound rather pompous? At this stage, do not stop to correct things or you will lose the big picture. Just make a mark in the margin. Have you got the balance right, spending most time on the most important points? Once you have read right through, wrestle with the awkward sentences. Be careful that any improvements you make do not introduce new errors. When you are sure you have done everything for your reader that you would like an author to do for you, you may proceed to the next stage.

Stage three

Do the mechanical bits in turn. Use the spellchecker but do your own check for things that it will miss, such as *it's/its*, *where/were*. A very common kind of mistake is to mistype the little words, for example *on* instead of *of*. Is your punctuation helpful? Work out all the sums, double check names and dates, physically look up everything that you have cross-referenced. When checking your grammar, common errors to look out for include verbs changing tense and pronouns drifting between *one* and *you*, sentences without verbs, run-on sentences where there should be a full stop in the middle, singular verbs with plural subjects and singular subjects with plural verbs.

Stage four

Give it to someone else to read, not necessarily a specialist in your subject. Ask them to make sure they can completely understand every sentence. In this way, they will test your own understanding. (Offer to do the same for them. You can learn a lot about your own writing from helping to make other people's writing clearer.)

Have a well-earned rest and look forward to an excellent mark. Then, when you get your essay back, resist the temptation to put it away in a file. Look at the comments carefully. If a few of you can get together and read each others' essays after marking you get a much better understanding of what makes a good essay in your subject.

ENGLISH LANGUAGE ESSAYS ARE SPECIAL

Different subjects are written about in different ways. This is partly because of the differing nature of subjects and partly as the result of traditions and conventions. History and literature essays, for example, are usually written in continuous prose. Science and technology essays will be interspersed with formulae and graphs. When you are writing an English Language essay, you may have to draw trees or graphs and you will need to use symbols. This means that you may not always be able to use continuous prose. You may even find it useful to adopt a report-writing style, using section headings as the author of the sample essay on page 221 has done. The emphasis is always on clear, effective communication.

You may be surprised to discover that, at least in the first year of a university course in English Language, students are not expected to be particularly innovative. There is a lot of groundwork to be learned before you are ready to produce original work.

Occasionally, students are worried because they feel they are not writing anything new but just reproducing what they have heard in lectures and read in books and articles, but essay writing in English Language is more than just a mindless copying out of facts. What the marker is looking for is the ability to handle all the information, to select the bits that answer the question and to put them together in a meaningful way. If you can do all that, you are demonstrating an understanding of the subject. Where you can use creativity and originality is in your selection of examples to illustrate the points you are making. If your examples are apt, the marker knows you have understood the concepts you are illustrating.

As you can see from the first part of this book, English Language embraces subjects of very different kinds. Some of them lend themselves to a very black and white, factual approach and others allow for more discussion. If you are more familiar with the discussion type of essay, you may think it an easier option, but this is not necessarily true. If you are answering on the history of English for example, you must remember that you are writing a language essay, not a history essay. If you are answering on sociolinguistics, you will not gain many marks for personal anecdotes; you must support your discussion of relevant points with evidence from sociolinguistic studies conducted in accordance with proper research methods. The content of the lecture courses will give you insights into what is relevant and important.

If you are answering a very general question on language, you could structure your essay into four sections dealing with the main topics of phonology (and how that relates to the spelling), morphology, syntax and vocabulary.

If you think you have a tendency to waffle, chose an essay

topic that focuses you on factual material. Again, the lectures are the best guide as to what to concentrate on.

COMPLETE DISASTER

What do you do if, in spite of all the good advice in this book, you fail to hand your essay in on time? You may have a good reason, such as illness. If so, you should provide a medical certificate. Your director of studies or personal tutor should be notified of serious personal problems which interfere with your work and they may be taken into account if you find you need an extension. Having three essays to hand in for the same day does not constitute grounds for an extension. It is merely a fact of university life and a very good reason for organising your time wisely. As soon as you feel you are behind schedule, have a word with your tutor.

If the worst comes to the worst, face up to it. Go to your tutor, lecturer or course organiser, own up and apologise. The longer you leave it, the harder it will be. Do *not* try to explain how your hard disk ate your essay at the last moment: you should have kept a floppy copy. *Nobody* believes that computers crash two hours before the submission time. By that late hour you should have a copy already printed out for a final proof read. You could hand that copy in if the computer crashes. Better to hand in a late draft than a draft late. You may find that you will be marked down for late submission but, if you have ignored all this advice, that is exactly what you deserve!

OTHER KINDS OF WRITING

Essays are most demanding pieces of writing that you will be asked to do in your first year. In later years, you may be asked to do a much longer dissertation and you may even want to write papers for conferences or articles for publication. Essay writing trains you for these activities. The processes are just the same. If you keep the needs of your reader in mind, you will be able to write for all occasions.

DO . . .

- Make yourself comfortable in a distraction-free zone.

- Use mindmaps, flow charts, and so on to help you make plans.

- Start writing as soon as you start researching.

- Try free writing or talking to get started or to unblock you if you get stuck.

- Ask for help if you need it.

FURTHER READING

P. Creme and M. Lea's *Writing at University: a guide for students* (1997), Open University Press, Buckingham is a very approachable general introduction to university writing.

The Student's Guide to the Internet 1998/9 by I. Winship and A. McNab (1998), Library Association Publishing, London is very helpful and easy to use but will date very quickly; keep an eye open for updated versions.

18 IMPROVING WRITTEN COMMUNICATION

Learning outcomes

- to start the lifelong task of learning to be a better writer

- to have some of the skills needed to be a good communicator

As you progress through university, you will have to deal with more and more complex concepts and your teachers will demand ever more exacting standards of precision and accuracy. Such rigour in your thinking will be reflected in your writing style. Here are a few hints on how to achieve depth without sacrificing clarity in your academic writing.

PARAGRAPHS

Topic sentences

You should have one topic or core idea per paragraph. It is a good idea to summarise it in a topic sentence.

The best place for the topic sentence is at the beginning of the paragraph because it makes for easy reading if your reader knows what you are writing about. If your reader is scanning through your work, the first sentence of each paragraph will catch the eye. You can put it at the end, which is also a position which gives emphasis, but that makes it harder work for the reader. Of course, if you really want to drive a point home, you can put it at both beginning and end.

As you write, keep your topic sentence in mind. When you find yourself straying from it, you should be on to the next paragraph.

Conversation

When you are writing, you are holding a conversation without being able to hear the other person. At the end of each paragraph, in a conversation, your partner would come in with a comment like:

What happened next?
Could you give me an example?
You have given me a whole lot of examples. Are you going to infer something?
Ah, but what if . . . ?
Are there any other ways of looking at this?
Say that again another way. I didn't understand a word of it!

If your paragraphs are well planned, your reader should be coming to same conclusion as you, just milliseconds before you state what has just become obvious. Or, at least, they will be formulating the question which your next paragraph is just about to answer. If you have experienced this in your reading, you will know how good it makes a reader feel.

Linking

In the best writing, one paragraph naturally and necessarily flows on to the next. Between paragraphs, take time to reflect:

• What did I establish in the last paragraph?

• How does my next paragraph relate to it?

In case the relationship is not immediately clear, it is helpful to have a few strategies ready to help you link paragraphs to each other.

For example, you could start with a paragraph which lists the topics to be discussed in the following paragraphs. You could end with a paragraph that summarises the preceding paragraphs. That may not be appropriate, if you are trying to follow an argument from beginning to end, in which case it might be helpful to have some signals ready to link paragraphs:

Enumerative: *Firstly . . . Secondly . . .Finally . . .*

Additive: *Another example . . . Furthermore . . . Moreover . . .*

Contrastive: *By contrast . . . On the one hand . . . On the other hand . . . Alternatively . . .*

When you are reading, make a note of any links which you think are effective and which you would feel comfortable using.

Beware, however, of overusing any of these links as they can easily become intrusive and irritating. Watch your writing very carefully for links that are becoming too much of a habit; *however* is one that many people pepper their work with.

The length of paragraphs should be varied. A long paragraph is hard reading and it is good to put in short, signpost ones, just to say where you have got to or where you are going, if you think you might be overloading your reader. The more important the point, the longer the paragraph, but an occasional, very short, punchy paragraph can be used very effectively to hammer home a vital point.

SENTENCES

The important thing about sentences is to keep the words in the right order. Do not alter the natural word order for rhetorical effect unless you really know what you are doing and you are really sure that your meaning will be made more rather than less clear.

The subject of the sentence goes at the beginning. It is no accident that the grammatical 'subject', the one that 'does' the verb, goes before the verb. The subject is what the sentence is about and the rest of the sentence is saying something about the subject. The second most conspicuous position in a sentence is at the end. Occasionally, it can be effective to build up to a climax at the end of a sentence.

A sentence is as long as it needs to be. If you are building complex relationships, your sentence might have to be very long but, if you keep the structure simple, a long sentence does not have to be difficult. Do not try to tuck too many additional bits of information into a sentence or your reader will lose the main thread. Too many short sentences sound rather ugly and fail to develop links and relationships but the very occasional short, sharp sentence can give a dramatic emphasis. Try to give your reader a bit of variety in sentence length.

Be impersonal . . .

. . . but know when to take responsibility for your own actions and opinions. Departments, and even individual lecturers, vary in their acceptance of the use of *I* in academic writing, but there is an increasing awareness outside universities that the use of the passive is a way of avoiding responsibility. 'The report could not be submitted before the meeting' actually means 'Oops, I missed the deadline'. When you want to make it clear that you are voicing a purely personal opinion, *I* is not only appropriate but essential: *It might be thought that . . . > I think . . .* (Not: *The author thinks . . .*)

Be active

Using the passive is a way of avoiding the use of *I*, but there is so much of the passive in academic prose that it becomes wearisome. Therefore, avoid it if you can.

It has been suggested by Smith . . . > Smith has suggested . . .

Be positive

Negatives can overstretch your readers' logical abilities:

There are no conditions under which the machine will not operate.
The elements of English grammar are not beyond 60 per cent of students.
Pressure must not be lowered until the temperature is not less that 40 degrees C.

Be brief

Word limits take into account the number of words necessary to deal with the set topic. Using unnecessary words for padding out or running over the limit does not make for a good essay or for pleasant reading. By how much can you shorten these examples?

A feature of much of this research is the illustration of . . .

There is continued, ongoing research . . .

Basically, the true facts may be said to be as follows: an undue and excessive proliferation of redundant and unnecessary modifiers and other repetitious or fairly weak insertions add very little or nothing to the meaningful impact of the discourse.

Be careful!

Sometimes you can be too brief:

Elephants do not require additional protection from buffalo.

Make sure that what goes together stays together:

Rabbit wanted for child with lop ears.

Sometimes you can say more than you intended:

The doctor said that he had never before seen this rare subcutaneous parasite in the flesh.

VOCABULARY

Jargon

One man's technical term is another man's jargon. In choosing your words, keep your target reader constantly in mind. When you are writing for your tutors and lecturers, you should be able to show that you have understood the technical terms and can use them correctly and appropriately.

Big words

Do not use big words where a little one will do the same job. If by *termination* you mean *end*, then use *end*. There is nothing to be gained by substituting *utilise* for *use*. There is a place for big words where they are the best ones to convey an accurate meaning, but they are not to be used unnecessarily for the sole purpose of sounding authoritative. You will just end up not knowing what you are talking about. Be especially self-disciplined about avoiding words whose meaning you are not completely sure about. Either consult a dictionary or use a word you know.

Rewrite the following in plain English:

1. *The noxious emissions from urban mobile sources are offensive to the olfactory organs.*

(This can be reduced to three words: answer at the end of the chapter.)

2. *Given a worst case scenario of initial non-achievement, essay, endeavour and endlessly maintain the pursuit of your aspirations.*

(The good writer's motto: answer at the end of this chapter.)

Formality

You need to maintain a certain level of formality. In selecting short, commonly used words, you must avoid any slang terms and colloquialisms.

Premodifiers

The build-up of long, heavily premodified, fluency-impairing noun phrases is a common failing in academic writing.

This could be rephrased:

Too many adjectives before a noun often impair the fluency of academic writing.

More verbs

Verbs make your text bounce along. Nouns and adjectives and prepositional phrases describing nouns are solid and slow your reader down. If you can use more verbs and fewer adjectives and nouns, you will sound much less boring:

After expulsion of the breath by the lungs . . .
After the lungs expel the breath . . .

You can increase the proportion of verbs to nouns by rewriting phrases like

make an adjustment to > adjust
come to the conclusion > conclude

Other examples which can be shortened to a single verb include:

arrive at a decision
make an examination of
conduct an investigation into

INFERENCE

In a real conversation, a lot of creativity comes from both sides. How many interpretations can you put on the following?

Where was I?
Are you on the phone?

These sentences work in conversation because you can rely on inference. You can give signals with your own facial expressions and other gestures. You alter your tone of voice. If an appropriate, unambiguous inference cannot be made, your hearer will ask what you mean. You can see if there is a blank or bewildered or angry or approving expression on a hearer's face. You can ask little 'tag' questions just to make sure the conversation is going as you intend. Right? When you write, you are deprived of all these safety checks.

You cannot assume that just because your reader is an expert in the subject, he or she will know what you mean anyway and reconstruct some sense from your half-expressed musings.

RHETORIC

Figures of speech are more likely to be found in writing where the purpose is to persuade or entertain than in the dispassionate prose of academic discourse. They should be used sparingly, but there are a few good tricks which are useful for getting your point across.

1. Simile

If you are going to use similes, choose ones which are really vivid. If you describe a parasite as looking *like a courgette seed*, you need to be sure your readers are readily familiar with courgette seeds.

2. Repetition

Usually, you go to quite a lot of effort to vary your sentence structure. A deliberate repetition of a pattern can therefore attract and hold the reader's attention.

I came. I saw. I conquered.

Why do bears, wishes and Billy Goats Gruff always repetitively come in threes? The universality of the number three in folklore testifies to its power. Here is another triplet:

Some books are to be tasted, some to be swallowed whole and some few to be chewed and digested. (Francis Bacon)

Here, the third time comes with a little extra. This is repetition and variation. Good writers have always exploited this device. Think of repetition with variation as the delivery of some weakening punches followed by the knock-out blow.

3. Rhetorical question

This can be very irritating if it is over-used. A useful strategy is to use a question as a topic sentence to open a paragraph, and then go on to answer it.

4. Climax

For maximum impact, make points in increasing order of importance so that the reader's interest grows to a peak. If you do it the other way round, the reader will be bored by mid-sentence. Similarly, always give your weakest examples or weakest arguments first and save the best for last.

PROFESSIONAL SPELLING

Spelling mistakes create a bad impression, especially when you make mistakes with technical terms specific to your subject; you undermine your readers' faith in your professional ability. Use your spellchecker to teach yourself spelling. If a word keeps coming up, take a moment to learn it. The academic writer always has a good dictionary to hand and uses it.

PUNCTUATION

Punctuation is not there for decoration but to help the reader. Too much punctuation can get in the way of fluent reading and if you put a piece of punctuation in the wrong place, it is obvious that you do not know what you are doing, whereas if you leave a piece of punctuation out it looks like a typing error. The lazy student will therefore follow the maxim: when in doubt, leave it out, and even the skilful student will use punctuation economically.

Full stops

Between the capital letter and the full stop there should be one, and only one, complete statement.

Commas

Commas separate lists. Note that there is no comma before the *and* in British English.

> *The colours of the rainbow are red, orange, yellow, green, blue, indigo and violet.*

Commas separate out non-essential bits (essential in upper case):

> *Suddenly,* THE DOOR SLAMMED.
> *Because the door slammed,* THE MAID SCREAMED.
> *Meanwhile, back at the ranch,* TONTO WAS, *with great skill,* MAKING PANCAKES.

Note how commas can change meaning. Compare

> *The chainsaw jugglers, who had been drinking before the show, beheaded themselves.*

with

*The chainsaw jugglers who had been drinking before the
show beheaded themselves.*

In the first sentence, the bit in commas is an optional extra
and all the jugglers in the sentence lost their heads. In the
second sentence, the beheaded jugglers are limited to those
who had been drinking. Think about the effect of adding
commas to:

*The students who are good at punctuation do well in
their essays.*

If a section in commas is, as here, in the middle of the sentence,
make sure your commas come in pairs.

Brackets

They come in pairs too.

Dashes

Dashes can be used in much the same way as commas and
brackets, for sectioning off an optional extra but they
should not be used to hang afterthoughts on to the end
of sentences.

Brackets and dashes can be useful if commas start nesting.
Compare

*Bad writers, who frequently compose long-winded sen-
tences, rendered, as this example shows, incomprehensible, more or less, to the average or even skilled reader,
by the interpolation of little, badly positioned, extra bits,
should be ostracised by the academic community.*

with

> *Bad writers (who frequently compose long-winded sentences, rendered – as this example shows – incomprehensible to the average, or even skilled reader, by the interpolation of little, badly positioned, extra bits) should be ostracised by the academic community.*

The second version is still dreadful, but not quite as nightmarish as the first.

Semicolons

If you feel that two sentences are so closely linked that you want to draw attention to the fact, you can use a semicolon instead of a full stop:

> *The students got very high marks; nothing in their answers was irrelevant to the question.*

Semicolons are also useful for lists where the items consist of more than one word, especially if the individual items contain commas:

> *I shared a flat with three exotic dancers from a Paris nightclub; a large, brown rat, who snored; a highly intelligent, but eccentric, philosophy student, called Alfie, who had a pet snake called Lucy; an ex-politician; and several cockroaches.*

Colons

You will notice how colons are used to introduce lists and examples in this book. They are also used to introduce quotations when no verb of saying is present.

Exclamation marks

Avoid them! They have very little place in academic discourse. And never, never, *never* use more than one at a time.

Hyphens

These can be useful for resolving ambiguities. Consider the difference between

> *extra-marital sex and extra, marital sex.*

Hyphens should also be used to avoid weird spellings: *de-ice* rather than *deice* and *go-between* rather than *gobetween.*

If you are not sure whether a compound word is hyphenated or not, and you cannot find it in your dictionary, make a decision and stick to it.

Quotation marks

Use quotation marks for short quotes but do not use them for 'iffy' words. If you think a word is not quite consistent with your formality level, find an 'un-iffy' word instead.

Apostrophes

Apostrophes are the punctuation marks that people seem to find hardest. In fact, they are really easy. In very formal writing, you will not use apostrophes for shortened words. *Do not write don't. It's it is, isn't it?*

Apostrophes are used to show possession:
If the possessor is singular, use *'s* (*the queen's crown*)
If the possessor is plural and ends in *-s*, use *'* (*cats' tails*)

If the possessor is plural and does not end in -s, use 's
(*men's heads*)
In other words, make the plural first and the possessive
second.

Special care is needed with personal names ending in -s such as
Robert Burns and *Charles Dickens*. There is a convention that
allows these names just to have an apostrophe: *Burns' poems*,
although *Burns's* possessive form may also be made safely in
the usual way by adding 's after the complete surname. It is a
common mistake to put the apostrophe inside the name:
Dickens' books are famous, but *Dicken's books* have been
written by the less well-known Mr Dicken.

If the possessor is a pronoun, do not use an apostrophe. You
would never dream of writing *hi's*, would you? The same goes
for *its*. *His head. Its tail.*

This is not all that there is to say about punctuation, but it
might be enough to prevent the commonest errors. When
checking your punctuation, the question to ask yourself is
always: 'Does it help the reader?'

ANSWERS TO BIG WORDS EXERCISES

1. City traffic stinks.
2. If at first you don't succeed, try, try, try again.

FURTHER READING

In addition to a good dictionary and thesaurus, you might like to
invest in one or two of the following, or find them in the library:

Hart's Rules for Compositors and Readers at the University Press Oxford (1983 edn)
is a compact manual with all you will ever need to know about abbreviations,
capitals, hyphens, italics, numerals, quotations, symbols, foreign phrases and so on.
It also has widely used proof-reading symbols. Every professional academic writer
should have one on their desk.

G. J. Fairburn and C. Winch get down to detail in *Reading, Writing and Reasoning* (1996) Buckingham: Open University Press. This is an excellent book.

J. Peck and M. Coyle provide help with the mechanics of writing in *The Student's Guide to Writing: Spelling, Punctuation and Grammar* (1999) Basingstoke: Macmillan.

Philip Gaskell combines a useful summary of the basics of good writing with some well-chosen examples of different styles in *Standard Written English* (1998) Edinburgh: Edinburgh University Press.

R. Quirk and S. Greenbaum's *A University Grammar of English* (1973) Harlow: Longman, is a useful book to refer to on occasion.

The Chicago Manual of Style (1993) Chicago: University of Chicago Press, is widely used as a standard reference book. It covers bookmaking and all you are ever likely to need on production and printing as well as giving a comprehensive and authoritative ruling on all matters of style.

6.4 WRITING SKILLS SELF-ASSESSMENT

When you have completed a piece of work – and also when you get a marked essay back from your tutor – measure it up on the table below. Note down your strengths and weaknesses. Now and again when you write, look back on your comments on earlier work. Have you taken your own criticisms on board?

First impression:
   Layout
   Word processing
   Attention to detail

Content:
   Definitions
   Adequate research
   Argumentation
   Evaluation
   Balance of argument
   Fairness of presentation
   Answering the question
   Overall integrity of structure

Paragraphs:
   Length
   Signposting
   Conversation
   Linking

Sentences:
   Length
   Clarity
   Grammar

Vocabulary:
   Consistent formality
   Accuracy
   Clarity

Spelling:

Punctuation:
   Accuracy
   Helpfulness

Other comments:

19 EXAMINATIONS

Learning outcomes

- to plan ahead

- to revise effectively

- to do your best on the day

- to learn from the experience

PREPARING FOR EXAMS

Look at past papers

Read the instructions. How many questions are you going to be asked? How many topics have you covered? How many topics to you need to revise? There may well be some bits of the course that you find easier or more absorbing than others. These are the ones to concentrate on. Just make sure that, if you are question spotting, you cover a safe amount of material. It is a good idea to have at least one spare topic in the bank in case one of your chosen subjects does not come up or the question is asked in a way you don't like.

Pick your questions carefully

If you have a talent for English Language and have worked hard all through the course, you will do well whatever questions you pick but if you lack confidence, there are some question types that can help you. It is possible to do really badly in an exam essay if you misread the question or wander off the point. You cannot stray from the point with exercise questions, like questions 2 and 8 in the sample exam paper on pages 211ff. With questions like these, you can see exactly where the marks are coming from. The same applies to sectioned, short-answer-type questions (like question 6). You might be asked for a definition of something you are not sure about, but you might manage to find something sensible to say about it and even if you do not, you can still get 80 per cent for getting all the rest right. You cannot get less than zero, so it is always worth making an attempt at an answer.

Plan your revision

You should be able to go over all your selected topics several times. Instead of planning to do one topic to death before going on to the next, aim to revise all your exam question topics once and then revise them all again, and again. That way, everything gets a fair turn and nothing gets skimped.

Revise

Instead of just reading over your notes, which can put you to sleep or make you think you're learning when you're not, try making notes of your notes and notes of the notes of your notes until you are down to a postcard's worth or less for each question. Then, check that you can expand it all again to exam-answer size. A glance at these notes before you go into the exam will give you all the confidence you need.

Do past papers

You might like to brainstorm a few past papers with friends to get ideas on how to structure answers, and at some point, when you are far enough on with your revision, but well before the examination date, set yourself a paper under exam conditions. The most frequently asked question is 'How much should I write?' and this is the best way to find out. How well can you fit your answers to the time allowed for each question? (See next paragraph.) You may be able to do exercise-type questions in less than the allotted time. Essay-type questions and definition-type questions, however, should take up all the time allowed. If you run out of things to say, you will have to go back to the books. Always learn more than you need, to allow for all the things that go straight out of your mind under the stress of the exam.

Do your sums

Three hours. Four questions. Three-quarters of an hour per question (maximum). Allow time for admin (like writing your name on each answer book), reading each question carefully, reading question again even more carefully, planning your answer. Forty minutes writing time, maximum.

  9.30 a.m. Start
10.05 a.m. *Think about finishing first question*
10.15 a.m. *Finish first question*
10.50 a.m. *Think about finishing second question*
11.00 a.m. *Finish second question*
11.35 a.m. *Think about finishing third question*
11.45 a.m. *Finish third question*
12.20 p.m. *Think about finishing fourth question*
12.30 p.m. *Smile.*

Calculations during exams to make the most of your timing are suggested in the hints on answers.

Look at more past papers

Now that you have the information needed to answer the questions, think how you would manipulate what you know to fit the different ways the questions are worded.

Make sure you know where and when the exam is

If you are not a morning person, get an alarm call or ask someone to see that you are up in time. You might be surprised by the number of people who sleep in on an exam morning.

ON THE DAY

(If you are unable to attend an exam, you must give your reason to the course organiser as soon as possible. If the reason is illness, you must produce a medical certificate.)

Get there in plenty of time so that you arrive feeling calm and confident, but do not get there too early; you do not want to hang about with a crowd of hysterical people working themselves into a nervous frenzy. Be sure you have everything you need: identification if required, watch, spare pens, handkerchief. If you want to, take a last look at your postcard-sized notes just to remind yourself that you really do know a lot. When you go into the examination hall, you will be asked to leave your notes, your coat and your bags at the back of the hall. Be sure to take your purse or your wallet with you.

The best cure for exam nerves is the knowledge that you have studied to the best of your ability. Remind yourself that you are as well prepared as you will ever be and look forward to showing off your knowledge. The examiners want you to pass and they are actively looking to reward you for displaying relevant knowledge. They are not going to try and catch you out. If nerves do begin to get the better of you, before or during the exam, breathe. Breathe very slowly and deeply, counting to seven (a lucky number) as you breathe in. Then see how slowly you can breathe out. Three breaths like this will have you perfectly calm.

Now read the instructions carefully. You will probably be asked to use a fresh examination book for each answer: remember to put your name on each book, and your tutor's name if it is asked for.

If there is anything you need to ask the invigilator, just put your hand up. It does occasionally happen that misprints occur on exam papers, in spite of careful proof-reading. If something is missed out from the instructions, or they are not clear, the invigilator will be glad to hear about it and will inform the rest of the class. If you run out of paper, feel unwell, need to go to the toilet, or need to borrow a pen, put your hand up and the invigilator will come to you.

Read through the questions and choose the ones you are going to do. Decide on the order in which you are going to do them. Make a note of the time at which you will need to start drawing each question to a conclusion. Make a note of the time at which you stop doing the each question, finished or not. Do not be tempted to overrun. Use any time left over to check through your answers, but do not start dithering and changing things that were right in the first place. If in doubt, go with your first instincts.

AFTER THE EXAM

When the exam is over, avoid people who ask, 'What did you write for question 2?'. It is over, finished, and there is nothing you can do to change it. Do not think about it again until you get the results. When you come out of an exam, you may still have a lot of left-over adrenalin. If you have two exams in one day, you need to come down to earth. Take a brisk walk, have something to eat and focus on the next exam.

When you get your exam back, even if you have done brilliantly, look at the examiner's remarks. Do you see where you went wrong?

Marks are most commonly lost because of:

• Not reading the instructions and doing one question too few or one too many.

• Not reading the question.

• Bad time management.

• Irrelevance.

- Trying to substitute made-up waffle for fact.

- Not giving enough examples.

Almost as importantly, do you see where and how you did well? Now you know what the examiners are looking for, make sure you give them more of it next time. Any problems, ask your tutor.

Stages of the examination process	Toolkit
Long-term preparation (Starting from the very beginning of the course or module)	• Collate your personal learning materials. • Copy the syllabus to which the examinations relate. • Look at past papers and try doing outline answers as you cover each topic. • Periodically, skim through your learning materials to keep them fresh in your mind.
Short-term revision (Two weeks before the examination)	• Summarise your notes. • Do the memory work – your notes, quotations, diagrams, symbols, definitions, etc. • Intersperse the memory work with exercises to test yourself.

On the day

- Arrive in a calm state.

- Read the instructions.

- Read the questions.

- Decide on which questions you are going to answer and the order in which you are going to answer them.

- Allocate your time.

- If you are answering an essay-type question, take time to write out a plan of your answer and think about essay structure.

- Keep checking to make sure you are really answering what the question asks.

- Keep checking your time to make sure you have a good go at each of your questions and leave none unanswered.

APPENDICES

I: SAMPLE DEGREE EXAM PAPER

This specimen paper is modelled on the kind of questions set at Edinburgh University. The actual content of the course is altered from time to time and other universities do not teach exactly the same things but it will give you some idea of the breadth of topics covered. There is something to appeal to every taste. If you are reading this before you start your course, remember that this is aimed at students who know a whole year's worth of English Language more than you do. It is not surprising that it looks quite hard in places. You will not find all the answers in this book. On the positive side, you will see that you really do have a wide choice of topics and you might even be able to tackle one or two of them already. Students sitting this exam will already know what topics they are best at and what type of questions suit them best.

This is a three hour exam. Students must do FOUR questions from the following:

1. How are vowels described and classified and in what way(s) does this method differ from that used for consonants?

2. Of the words given below, list the ones that begin with . . .
   a) a voiced fricative phoneme
   b) an approximant phoneme
   c) a voiceless stop phoneme
   d) a bilabial phoneme
   e) a voiceless dental phoneme.

Honest, sprite, judge, plan, blip, those, veal, fly, blink, wind, jack, shin, hat, rig, mind, sue, zoo, vine belt, prime, thank, lime, deal, wrist, frame, aid, name, mime, rough, throng, frank, middle, pill, tramp, found, ramp, row, own, full, vile, thought, this, toll, the, think, you, dip, noon, zeal, sin.

3. 'The borrowing of loan words from languages like Latin, Scandinavian, French, Dutch etc., into English at various points in its history has served merely to increase the lexicon of English.' Do you agree with this statement? Give examples to support your argument.

4. Discuss the claim that, in phonological terms, the Southern Hemisphere varieties of English are more closely related to RP than they are to General American.

5. How would you distinguish a Glaswegian Scots speaker from an Aberdonian Scots speaker **and** what features (over and above the usual features of SSE) would you expect them to share?

6. Drawing examples from the accents of English, explain all of the following terms:
   a) phoneme and allophone
   b) 'true' diphthong
   c) non-rhotic accent
   d) Scots and Scottish Standard English
   e) lexical difference between accents.

7. Why is it important in the syntactic analysis of English sentences to distinguish between 'categories' and 'functions'?

8. Analyse the syntactic structures of the following sentences:
   a) Sheila made her friends very happy.
   b) The landlord made Fred a nice sandwich.

c) The poor old man was really burnt again.

d) You should look at this particular sentence very carefully.

e) Nothing will stop his meteoric rise to the top.

9. Discuss some of the similarities and differences between derivational and inflectional morphology.

10. What kinds of evidence can you produce to suggest that women's pronunciation is more sensitive to social class than that of men?

11. What do you understand by the phenomenon of *accommodation* between the speech of individuals of different social classes, regional dialect speakers and even nationalities?

12. 'The meaning of language is to a large extent determined by its use in actual contexts.' Discuss with examples.

13. Using the data from either OR both of the following passages, illustrate what can be learned concerning the details of vowel and consonant pronunciation in the second half of the sixteenth century.

a) Ei bi-līv in God ðe fāðr aul-mih-ti, mākr ov he-vn and erþ, and in dʒe–zuz Krist hiz uonli sun our lord. Huitʃ uas kon-se-vd bei ðe hol-li gōst bōrn ov ðe vir-dʒin Mā-ri. Suf-ferd undr pons pei-lat, uas criu-si-feid, ded and biu-ri-ëd, hi des-sen-ded in-tu hel. ðe þird de- hī rōz agēn from ðe ded. Hi as-sen-ded intu hēvn, and sitþ on ðe riht hand ov God ðe fādr aul-mih-ti. From ðens hi ʃaul kum tu dʒudʒ ðe kuik and ðe ded. Ei bi-līv in ðe hol-li gōst, ðe hol-li ka-þo-lik tʃurtʃ, ðe kom-mu-ni-on of sēnts, ðe for-giv-nes of sinz. ðe re-zur-rek-si-on ov ðe bod-di. And ðe leif evr-last-ing. So bi it.

b) The sam day a-ffor non landyd at the Towre wharf the Kynges lord of myssrulle, and ther mett with hym the Shreyffes lord of mysrulle with ys men, and every on

havyng a rebynd of bluw and whytt a-bowt ther nekes,
and then ys trumpet, druws, mores dansse, and tabrett,
and he toke a swaerd and bare yt a-fore the kynges
lord of mysrulle for the lord was gorgyusly arrayed in
purprelle welvet furyd with armyn, and ys robe braded
with spangulls of selver full; and a-bowt ym syngers,
and a-for hym on gret horses and in cottes and clokes
of . . . in-brodered with gold and with balderykes a-
bowt ther nekes, whytt and blue sarsnets, and chynes
of gold, and the rest of ys servands in bluw gardyd
with whytt, and next a-for ys consell in bluw taffata
and ther capes of whytt . . . ys trumpeters, tabers,
drums, and flutes and fulles and ys mores dansse,
gunes, mores-pykes, bagpipes; and ys mass . . . and
ys gayllers with pelere, stokes, and ys axe, gyffes, and
boltes, sum fast by the leges and some by the nekes,
and so rod thrugh Marke lane and so thrugh Graysus
strett and Cornhylle; and . . . trompet blohyng, making a proclamasyon . . . and so the kynges was cared
from the . . . skaffold; and after the shreyffes lord;
and the kynges lord gave the shreyffes lord a gowne
with gold and sylver, and anon after he knelyd downe
and he toke a sword and gayff ym iij strokes and mad
ym knyght, and after thay drank on to thodur a-pon
the skaffold, and ys cofferer casting gold and sylver in
every plase as they rod, and after his coffrer ys carege
with hys cloth-saykes on horsseback; and so went a-
bowt Chepe, with ys gayllers and presonars; and
afterwards the ij lordes toke ther horssys and rode
unto my lord mare to dener; and after he came bake
thrugh Chepe to the crosse, and so done Wodstrett
unto the shreyffes howse for mor than alff a nore, and
so for the the Olde Jury and London wall unto my lord
tresoreres plasse, and ther they had a grete banket the
spasse of alffe a nore; and so don to Bys-shopgate and
to Ledenhall and thrughe Fanchyrche strett, and so to
the Towre warffe; and the shreyffes lord gohynge with
hym with torche-lyght, and ther the kynges lord toke

ys pynnes with a grett shott of gonnes, and so the
shreyffes lord toke ys leyffe of hym and cam home
merele with ys mores dansse danssyng and so forth.

(Diary of Henry Machyn, Citizen and Merchant Tay-
lor of London: 1552–3)

14. What kind of source materials are available to us for the
recovery of the pronunciation of English in the sixteenth
and seventeenth centuries?

15. What linguistic characteristics of the following passage
suggest that it is written in Middle Scots?

   1 Ane wedow dwelt intill ane drop thay dayis
     Quhilk wan hir fude of spinning on hir rok;
     And na mair had, forsuth, as the fabill sayis
     Except of hennis scho had ane lytill flok;
   5 And thame to keip scho had ane jolie cok,
     Richt courageous, that to this wedow aye
     Devydit nicht and crew befoir the day.

     Ane lytill fra this foirsaid wedowis hous
     Ane thornie schwa thair wes of greit defence,
  10 Quhairin ane foxe, crafty and cautelous,
     Maid his repair and daylie residence,
     Quhilk to this wedow did greit violence
     In pyking off pultrie baith day and nicht,
     And na way be revengit on him scho micht . . .

  15 'Quhen I behald your fedderis fair and gent,
     Your beik, your breist, your hekill and your came –
     Schir, be my saull and the blessit sacrament,
     My hart warmys: me think I am at hame.
     Yow for to serve, I wald creip on my wame
  20 In froist, in snaw, in wedder wan and weit,
     And lay my lyart loikkis under your feit.'

With that the cok, upon his tais hie
Kest up his beik and sang with all his mycht.
Quod Schir Lowrence, 'Weill said, sa mot I the:
25 Ye ar your faderis sone and air upricht!
Bot of his cunning yit ye want ane slicht,
For,' quoth the tod, 'He wald, and haif na dout,
Baith wink and craw and turne him thryis about.'

16. What kinds of attempt were made in the eighteenth
century at the standardisation and 'fixing' of pronunciation? What part was played in particular by the use of
specialised alphabets?

17. Describe some of the attitudes to and the characteristics of
eighteenth century 'Scotch' pronunciation.

18. Describe and discuss, with examples, the language of one
OR two kinds of Scots dialect literature written in the
twentieth century.

Hints on answers

1. You could make a reasonable attempt at question 1. The
answer to this would show how vowels are described in
terms of high or low; front or back; rounded or un-
rounded. You would need to explain what these terms
mean and give examples. Consonants are described in
terms of manner and place of articulation and whether
they are voiced or voiceless. You would also need to
distinguish between oral and nasal consonants. Again,
everything you say must be backed up with examples.
Draw diagrams.

2. This would be a good one to do first. Students who have
practised this type of question can save a lot of time here.
No essay plan is required. There is no time wasted on
thinking of the best way to express yourself. The only

danger is overconfidence leading to silly mistakes. So use some of the time you have saved to check your work carefully. You have enough information to get full marks in this question. Have a go with the help of Chapter 1 and then check your answers.

a) *those, veal, zoo, vine, vile, this, the, zeal*

b) *honest, wind, rig, lime, wrist, aid, rough, ramp, row, own, you*

c) *plan, prime, pill, tramp, toll*

d) *plan, blip, blink, wind, mind, belt, prime, mime, middle, pill*

e) *thank, throng, thought, think*

3. The wording of this question suggests you might want to disagree with the statement. Yes, of course borrowing from these languages (give examples from each) has increased the number of words we have at our disposal, both directly and indirectly by giving us a lot of new derivational morphemes, but it has done a lot more besides. We have a different vocabulary for each register (informal – native and words of Scandinavian origin; literary – French; learned – Latin). We have a lot of dialectal variation which came about because of the different kinds of contact with other languages in various parts of Britain. We also have changes in orthography, phonology and, to a lesser extent, syntax. By the time you explain and expand all this with good examples, you have at least a forty-minute essay. A student who does question 2 efficiently gains some extra time and could use some of it here.

4. You will be able to find out a bit about South African, Australian and New Zealand Englishes from the essay on page 221. You can see that the exam question expects you to cover the similarities between these and General American, as well as pointing out the differences and producing a balance of evidence in favour of their greater similarity to RP. This requires a well-structured essay-type answer, with the correct use of terminology, correct use of

brackets and plenty of examples. See the sample essay comparing RP with Southern Hemisphere Englishes. You would hardly expect an exam answer to be as polished as this but it will give you some idea of the level of knowledge required.

5. Again an essay-type answer in two main sections. You could use the subheadings of phonology, lexis, inflectional morphology and syntax as subheadings (even if morphology and syntax are likely to be very short). If you have four main paragraphs, that means about ten minutes per paragraph, a bit more for phonology and lexis, a bit less for morphology and syntax. Leave a few blank lines between each paragraph in case you suddenly remember a key feature that you have forgotten to mention.

6. Questions in sections like this are safer than essay answers. Even if you get one bit wrong, you can still get the rest right. If you are not good at sticking to the point, this kind of question keeps you focused. Unless there is anything to tell you otherwise, assume that each section is equally weighted. Five parts, eight minutes per part.

7. You might not have enough information to answer this yet but you could begin to think about it. A 'noun' is a word category but think how many 'functions' it can have in a sentence. It can be the headword of the subject noun phrase. It can be the headword of the object noun phrase. It can be part of a prepositional phrase. What else can it do? What can adverbs do? What can participles do?

8. To answer this question, all you need to do is draw some trees and note any interesting features. You can collect a lot of marks here, quite quickly, if you have had lots of practice. You might not need eight minutes per tree. Again, you might like to answer this question first and then you can reallocate the time you save.

9. This is as near as you get to a 'tell me all you know about. . .' type of question. Take a moment to think about structure. What can you do with derivational affixes? You can change meaning and you can change class. What can you do with an inflectional suffix? Deal with nouns and pronouns then take a new section deal with verbs. What do they have in common? You could talk about allomorphy here.

10. This looks like an opportunity to waffle, but beware. To answer this you would need to have looked at a few sociolinguistic studies. You could summarise the results of these studies by drawing free-hand graphs and go on to discuss what the figures show.

11. As with the last question, this cannot be answered on the basis of anecdotal guesswork. You would need to refer to properly conducted field studies.

12. The best way to answer this question is to come up with some really good examples that give you plenty to say.

13. When faced with a text question, resist the temptation to start at the beginning and work your way through word by word. The question itself suggests a more structured approach. Look for evidence of vowel pronunciation. Then deal with consonants.

14. The spelling reformer and naïve speller texts provided for the previous question give you a flying start in this one. You would then go on to other evidence such as rhymes, puns, foreign phrase books, etc. – with examples of course – and evaluate the reliability of the evidence they provide.

15. Another text question. Think paragraphs: orthography, phonology, lexis, inflectional morphology and syntax. By the time you find a few things to say about each of these, you will have quite a substantial essay.

16. It seems that some people have always got to be telling other people how to speak properly! This subject has not been covered in this book because of lack of space, but the earlier elocution teachers provide fascinating reading.

17. During the Scottish Enlightenment, educated Scots went to great lengths to get rid of any trace of Scots from their speech and writing. It was said of David Hume, the philosopher, that he died confessing not his sins but his Scotticisms. The examiner would be looking for a balanced account of the suppression of Scots with some reference to writers and contemporary commentators.

18. Try making your own outline of the ideal exam answer. Even if you know nothing about Scots dialect literature, you could suggest some essential paragraph headings for discussing language.

II: SAMPLE ESSAY WITH MARKER'S COMMENTS

A detailed comparison of Received Pronunciation and the major varieties of Southern Hemisphere English

Introduction

This essay will look at the similarities and differences between Received Pronunciation and the major varieties of Southern Hemisphere English, namely Australian, New Zealand and South African English, taking into account the vowel systems and various other features of the accents.

Received Pronunciation

Received Pronunciation (RP) is an accent of English with no regional definition – it is non-localisable, although it does originate historically from southeast England. RP can be found throughout Britain, amongst the upper and upper-middle classes. It is also known as BBC English, as it is the accent of most BBC newsreaders and is used in the majority of the private sector of the education system, as well as being used as the model for learning English as a foreign language.

No more

Not everywhere. Certainly not in the USA.

According to <u>Wells (1984</u>), there are a
number of variations of RP: Mainstream RP, the central tendency; U-RP
or Upper Class RP; Adoptive RP, spoken by adults who did not speak RP as
children, due to a change in social circumstances; and Near RP, which is not
exactly RP, but is very similar and is
also non-localisable.

Page number?

Southern Hemisphere English

The Australian and New Zealand Accents are very similar to each other,
except in a <u>couple of respects</u>. South
African English is also similar to Australian but with a number of important
differences. All three accents reflect the
development that had taken place in the
south of England up to the <u>beginning of
the nineteenth century when the territories were settled from Britain and the
English language established</u>. Since then
the territories have developed their own
characteristic accents.

[the marker has
underlined this without
further comment.]

How do you know
this? Refs.

Neither Australian and New Zealand
English show much geographical variation – except in the Southernmost provinces of New Zealand, where, <u>due to
the Scottish influence, the accent is rho-
tic</u>. Accent variability in both countries
is social and stylistic rather than geographical (Wells 1984). According to
Mitchell and Delbridge (1965), there
are three main types of pronunciation
in present day Australian and New

Says who?

Zealand English: Cultivated, which is the most similar to RP; General, where the vowels have undergone a diphthong shifting; and Broad, which is similar to General and has extra duration in the first element of the diphthong.

South African English does show some regional variation, but it can also be divided into three main types: Conservative, which differs <u>very slightly</u> from RP; *e.g.?* Respectable, which has more extensive differences; and Extreme, or Broad, which is distinct from both Conservative and Respectable South African English. What is unusual about South African English is that it is spoken, as a first language, by only a <u>very small minority of the population</u>, none of whom belong *Evidence?* to the manual labouring class. Therefore, even though there is a Broad South African accent, it is <u>not really comparable</u> to *why?* Broad Australian English, spoken by members of the lower working class.

RP Vowels

RP has six pairs of vowels. /iːɪ e ɛ u ʊ ɔ ʌ ɔ ɒ ɑ a/, three '<u>true</u>' diphthongs /ɔɪ aɪ aʊ/ and *Why are they called* three centring diphthongs /ɪə ɛə ʊə/. *this?* The pairs of vowels are made up of 'short' vowels and 'long' vowels – although the duration of both long and short vowels does vary depending on the phonetic environment. Short vowels do *This could be* not occur in a stressed monosyllable with *expressed more clearly.* no final consonant and <u>Wells (1984)</u> *Page?*

labels these vowels 'checked' – because they are always followed by a consonant which 'checks' the pulse of air from the vowel, as in *fit* /fɪt/ and *cup* /kʌp/. Long vowels and diphthongs can occur in a stressed syllable with no final, checking consonant – and are therefore labelled 'free', although they can also occur in the same environment as checked vowels.

One very notable feature of RP is that it is a broad-BATH accent (Wells 1984). This means that in the BATH set of words, RP uses the stressed vowel /ɑː/ where many other accents use the /æ/ vowel and are known as 'flat-BATH' accents/

Back/front contrast

Australian and New Zealand Vowels

The Australian and New Zealand vowel systems are similar to RP in that they all contain the same number of phonemes; but realisationally the systems are notably different.

All the high long vowels are realised as diphthongs:

/i/ > [ɪi] ~ [əɪ]   /u/ > [u] ~ [əʊ]
/e/ > [ɛɪ] ~ [ʌɪ]   /o/ > [əʊ] ~ [ʌʊ]

And the front short vowels are all realised significantly higher than in RP and usually higher in New Zealand than in Australian.

/a/ > [æ] ~ [ɛ] (Aus)   /ɛ/ > [e]   /ɪ/ > [i] (Aus)
   [ɛ] (NZ)   [ə] ~ [ɪ] (NZ)

The most important phonological difference between Australian and New Zealand English is the differing realisations of the KIT (or *bit*) vowel /ɪ/, Where the Australian vowel is realised higher than the RP one, the New Zealand vowel is realised centrally rather than high.

<u>Australian and New Zealand are, in general broad-BATH accents</u>, like RP; although some speakers do use the TRAP vowel /æ/ in some words of the BATH set – where the vowel is followed by a nasal plus another consonant (Wells 1984), as in *advantage*.

Are they really?

It is much more complex than this.

The New Zealand short vowel system differs from both the RP and Australian systems in that it has only two phonologically significant degrees of height (Wells 1984). It has two front vowels /e æ/, two central vowels /ə ʌ/, and two back vowels /ʊ ɒ/.

Australian does not distinguish between the weak vowels /ə/ and /ɪ/ in all environments except before a velar (Wells 1984). This means that, unlike in RP, there is no distinction between *boxers* and *boxes* [bɒksəz]; and that the weak form of *it* [ət] and *is* [əz] are phonetically identical with *at* and *as*.

Watch out: the claim that AE has no regional variation – is there social variation?

South African Vowels

South African English, like RP, as well as Australian and New Zealand

accents, has distinctive vowel length
(Giegerich 1992). It does not however
have the distinctive vowel quality that is
present in RP.

South African high, long vowels /i/ and
/u/ are not diphthongised to the same   Are they at all? If so
extent as they are in Australian, New   under what conditions?
Zealand or even RP accents. In Broad
South African they remain as monophthongs, becoming very narrow
diphthongs in the Respectable and Con-   Define
servative accents.

The BATH vowel /ɑː/ is a very back   Raised? What is it?
vowel – more back than the RP vowel   [ɒː]?
and contrasting with the front vowel /æ/
found in Australian and New Zealand
English. Other long vowels have similar
realisations to long RP vowels.

The short front vowel /ɪ/ (KIT) has undergone a phonemic split in South African English (Wells 1984) and constitutes
a unique feature of the accent (Giegerich   Always put in page
1992). In stressed syllables, adjacent to   reference as well.
velar consonants, the relatively high
front vowel [ɪ] occurs, as it does word-
initially and after /h/. Elsewhere the   Describe the features
vowel [ï] occurs, which in most South   of this. What does ¨
African accents has no contrast with [ə].   mean?

Most other short vowels in South African are realised similarly to RP short
vowels, although /e/ and /æ/ tend to be
closer in South African English than
they are in RP, more like those of Australian and New Zealand English.

RP /r/

RP is a non rhotic accent – /r/ cannot occur in the syllable rhyme. Where rhotic accents have a rhyme /r/, RP tends to have a centring diphthong. Although /r/ cannot occur in the syllable rhyme in RP, intervocalic /r/ does occur in the middle of words and in word-final position when the following word begins with a vowel – where it is known as linking /r/.

Intrusive /r/ is another feature of RP – one without historical reasoning. This /r/ is unetymological, occurring after /ɪə ə/ and various other vowels at a word boundary when the next word begins with a vowel, as in *the idea isn't* /ðiː aɪdɪərɪznt/. Intrusive /r/ also occurs in the middle of words such as *gnawing* /nɔːrɪŋ/ (Wells 1984).

> What do you mean?

Australian, New Zealand and South African /r/

All three southern hemisphere accents of English are, like RP, non-rhotic, with the exception of the southern provinces of New Zealand and those accents of South African which are Afrikaans influenced.

> Why do you assume that SA [r] is an Afrikaans 'influence'?

I

The /r/ phoneme in Australian and New Zealand is very similar to its RP counterpart – occurring in the same environments as both linking and intrusive /r/. This is usually the approximant [ɹ]. In South African English, however, the /r/ phoneme is usually an obstruent: either a tap [ɾ]

(intervocalically, after a velar plosive or
/θ/) or a *post-alveolar fricative*[ɹ] (in the
clusters /tr dr/ and word initially). South
African English also follows the RP
model for intrusive and linking /r/,
although it often uses a glottal stop
instead (Wells 1984).

Other RP Features

There are a number of features, apart
from those covered already, which distinguish RP from other accents (Wells 1984).
One is Place Assimilation, particularly
associated with casual speech – where
the final consonant of one word is affected
by the first consonant of the following
word, i.e. ten minutes /tɛmmɪnɪts/. Another common feature of RP is Elision,
again associated with fast casual speech –
where the consonant clusters are reduced,
as in next day /nɛksdeɪ/. One final, very
common, feature of mainstream RP is
that of Smoothing – where diphthongs
in a prevocalic environment are realised
as monophthongs, as in player [pleː ə].

*I suspect this happens
in FRP too.*

Not in AE?

Other Australian, New Zealand and South African Features

The feature T Voicing occurs in all three
varieties of southern hemisphere English
– that is, the neutralisation of the opposi-
tion between /t/ and /d/. It occurs in the
environment V_V and results in an
alveolar tap [ɾ] in free or stylistic variation
with [t] (Wells 1984).

So is it T voicing?

The Australian and New Zealand /l/ is
dark, possibly pharyngealised at times,
in all environments – there is <u>no clear</u>   Debateable
<u>and dark /l/ distinction.</u>

Conclusion

There are a large number of similarities,
most of which have been identified in
this essay, between RP and the southern
hemisphere varieties of English mainly
due to the fact that the Britons who first
settled in Australia, New Zealand and
South Africa were predominantly from
those areas from which RP originates.
The differences – and there are a large
number of these also – stem from the fact
that in the two hundred years since colonisation the accents have had a chance
to develop their own characteristics
without the influence of a predominant
accent such as RP.

Bibliography

Giegerich, H. J. (1992) *English Phonology: An intro-
duction*, Cambridge: Cambridge University Press.
Mitchell, A. G. and Delbridge, A. (1995) *The Speech of
Australian Adolescents: A survey*, Sydney: Angus
and Robertson.
Wells, J. C. (1984) *Accents of English 1: an introduc-
tion*, Cambridge: Cambridge University Press.
Wells, J. C. (1984) *Accents of English 2: the British
Isles*, Cambridge: Cambriedge University Press.
Wells, J. C. (1984) *Accents of English 3: Beyond the
British Isles*, Cambridge: Cambridge University
Press.

INDEX

abstract noun, 40–1
accentual verse, **128**
accentual-syllabic verse, **128**
accommodation, **100–1**
accusative, 30, 66–7
active voice, **54**
adjective, 22, 23, 26, 33, 42–3, 135–6
adjective phrase, 51, 52
adverb, 22, 43,57, 109
adverbial, 57, 67–8, 69
advertising, **113**
affixation, 22, 24–7, 65, 89, 119–20
affricate, **8**
age, **99–100**
alliterative poetry, **127**
allomorphy, 25–6, 31, 35, 37
allophone, 13, 85
alveolar, **8**
American English, 86, 91, 92–3, 98
analogy, **124**
anapaest, **129**
anaphoric reference, 108, 112
Anglo-Saxon *see* Old English
antonymy, **16–17**
apparent time, 100
approximant, 7, **8**
aspect, **53–4**, 73
assonance, **127**
auxiliary verb, **53–6**, 73

back (vowel), **10–11**
base, **24**
bilabial, **8**
Black English, **142**
blend, **20**
bound (morpheme), 23, 24

caesura, **132**
case, 29, 30, 31, 66–7
cataphoric reference, **108**
central consonant, **9**
Central French, 70, 71, 118
central vowel, **10–11**
chain shift, **123**
Chomsky, Noam, 39
class changing (affix), **24**
class maintaining (affix), **24**
clause, 44, 111
clipping, **19–20**
close (vowel), **10**
Cockney, 86
cohesion, 107–9
collocation, 17, 109
common noun, **41**
competence, **39**
complement, 50–3, 57
complex transitive verb, **51–2**, 54
compound, 23, 65
concrete noun, **41**
concrete poetry, **134–5**
conjugation class words, 34–7, 67, 69, 75, 92

conjunction, 44, 109, 111, 112, 135, 136
conjunction (cohesive), 109
consonance, 127
consonant, 6–9
constituent, 46–9, 136
context, 140
convergence, 101
conversation, 110
conversion, 26
co-ordinating conjunction, 44
count noun, 33, 41, 45
Creoles, 142–4
cumulation, 34, 37

dactyl, 129
dative, 30, 66–7
declension class words, 29–33, 66–7, 69, 75, 91
definite article, 44–5, 135
degree adverb, 43
deixis, 140
demonstrative, 44–5
density (of network), 103
dental, 8
derivational morphology see grammatical word formation
determiner, 33, 44, 90–1
dialect, 82
dictionaries, 76–7
dimeter, 129
diphthong, 12
dipode, 131
ditransitive verb, 51, 54
divergence, 101

Early Modern English, 72–6
ellipsis, 108–9
empty tense marker, 74
endocentric compound, 23
end-stopping, 132

enjambment, 132
eponym, 18–19
euphemism, 21
exocentric compound, 23

finite (verb), 34, 55
foot, 129
FOOT/STRUT split, 76
formality level, 100
free (morpheme), 23
fricative, 7, 9
front (vowel), 10–11
functional shift, 26

gender, 66, 124
gender of speaker, 98–9
general class (noun), 31–2
genitive, 30, 31, 67
gerund see verbal noun
glottal, 8, 86
grammatical word formation, 17, 22–7, 119–21
grammetrics, 135–6
graphology, 107, 111, 127
great vowel shift, 72, 75, 123

head(word), 23, 44, 57–8
hexameter, 129
high (vowel), 10–11
Highland English, 85
horoscopes, 107, 112
hypercorrection, 102
hypernym, 17
hyponym, 16–17

iambic, 129
imperative, 35, 107, 112, 140
indefinite article, 44
indicative, 35
indicator (sociolinguistic), 102
inference, 140

infinitive, 35, 56, 77
inkhorn controversy, 73
intensive verb, 52
International Phonetic
    Alphabet, 6
interrogative, 124
interrogative pronoun, 42
intransitive verb, 50, 69
intrusive /r/, 87
invariant class (noun), 32
invariant verb, 35

labio-dental, 8
language acquisition, 141–2
language planning, 144
lateral (consonant), 9
Latin, 32, 65–6, 69, 70, 71,
    77–8, 118–19, 119–21
levelling, 124
lexical cohesion, 109
lexical item, 17, 22, 23
lexical variation, 83, 87, 93
linking /r/, 86–7
lip rounding, 10
lip spreading, 10
loan, 18, 65, 69, 70, 71, 73,
    88–9, 116–19

made-up word, 21
main clause, 44
manner of articulation, 7, 9
mass noun, 33, 41, 45
merger, 112
metaphor, 21
metre, 128–33
Middle English, 68–72
mixed class (noun), 32
mixed verb, 35
modal verb, 34, 54–6, 90,
    112
modifier, 42, 43, 57, 112

monotransitive verb, 50–1, 54,
    69
mood, 34, 35, 54–6
morpheme, 22–7, 31

nasal (consonant), 9
negative, 54, 68, 70, 73, 77–8,
    89, 124
network (sociolinguistic), 103
newspapers, 107, 113
nominal, 48, 58
nominative, 30, 31, 67
non-count noun see mass noun
non-finite (verb), 34, 35–6,
    55–6
non-grammatical word
    formation, 17, 18–22
normal non-fluency, 110
Norman French, 68, 69, 118
Northern English, 10, 63, 76,
    87, 88, 93
noun, 22, 23, 26, 31, 40–1,
    66–7
noun phrase, 42, 44, 48, 49–
    50, 51, 57, 109, 111, 135–6
number, 29, 30, 31, 34, 66–7
numeral, 45

object, 49, 51, 67
object predicative, 49, 51
oblique, 30, 31
observer's paradox, 101
Old English, 62–8
onomastics, 144–5
onomatopoeia, 20
open (vowel), 10
oral (consonant), 9
orthoepists, 75–6

palatal, 8
palato-alveolar, 8

part of speech *see* word class
passive participle, **54**, *56*
passive voice, **54**, *56*, 70, 112, 125
past participle *see* perfect participle, passive participle
pentameter, **129**
perfect aspect, **54**, *56*, 74
perfect participle, 36, **54**, *56*, 92, 136
performance, **39**
person, 29, 30, 34, 55
personal pronoun, 30, **42**, 45, 69
phoneme, 4, 10, **12–13**, 22, 64
phonemic variation, 82, **83–5**
phonetic variation, **82**
phonetics, **3**
phonology, **3**
phonotactic variation, 82, **86–7**, 122–3
pidgins, **142–3**
place of articulation, 7, **8**
plexity (of network), **103**
plosive, 7, **9**
post-alveolar, **8**
pragmatics, **139–40**
predicate, **46–7**, 48
prefix, 22, **24–7**, 89
preposition, **43–4**, 48, 69
prepositional phrase, **44**, 49, 51, 52, 57, 109
prepositional verbs, **52**
present participle, 36, **53–4**, *56*, 136
progressive aspect, **53–4**, *56*
pronoun, 30, **41–2**, 50, 112
proper noun, **41**

quantifier, **45**

real time, **100**
realisation *see* allophone
realisational variation, 82, **85–6**
Received Pronunciation (RP), **83–7**, 93, 97
reference *see* anaphoric, cataphoric
reflexive pronoun, **42**, 99
register *see* formality level
relative pronoun, **42**
rhoticity, **75–6**, 78–9, **86–7**, 93, 98, 143
rhyme, **127**
rhyme scheme, **133**
rhyming slang, **20**
root, **23–4**, 120–1
runes, **64**

salience, **101–2**
Scandinavian, 63, 66, 69, 71, 116–17
schwa, **11**
scientific or technical language, **112**
Scots, 77, 82, **88–92**
Scots Vowel Length Rule, **84–5**
Scottish Standard English (SSE), 12, **82–91**, 97, 122
semantics, **16**
Shetland, **88**
silent stress, **131**
simple aspect, **53**
social class, **97**
social network, **103**
sonnet, **133**
Southern Hemisphere Englishes, **93**, 221–9
split, **112**
stanza, 127, **133–5**
stop, **9**

stress, **128–9**, 136
stress-timing, **129**
strong verb, 35, 36, 67
subject, **46–7**, 67
subject predicative, 49, 52
subjunctive, 35
subordinate clause, 44, 67, 69, 111, 112
subordinating conjunction, 44
substitution, 108
suffix, 22, **24–7**, 89, 119–20
suppletion, 33, 35
suppletive verb, 35, 36
syllabic verse, 128
syncretism, 30, 31, 34, 36, 124
synonymy, **16–17**

tags, 110
tense, **34–5**, 55
tetrameter, **129**
TH-variable, **103–4**
Tok Pisin, 142–3

transferable skills, **xiii, xiv**
trimeter, **129**
trochee, **129**

variable (sociolinguistic), **102**
v-deletion, 70
velar, **8**
verb, 26, 41, 111, 136
verb phrase, 49, **50–7**
verbal noun, 36
vocal tract, 6
voice, 54
voicing, **7–8**
vowel, **9–12**

weak class (noun), **32**
weak verb, 35
Wessex, 88
word class, **40–5**
World Englishes, 73, **142**

zero morpheme derivation, 26